The Safe Money System®

Uncommon Wisdom to Secure Your Retirement
—Without Wall Street's Risk

RANDY HAMMON
Founder My Retirement Coach, Inc.

2nd Edition, August 2011

ISBN: 978-0-615-55748-9

Library of Congress Number: 2010920163

Graphic design by Nolan Hammon

www.nolanhammon.com

Printed in the U.S.A.

"Buying stocks or bonds is gambling. You're betting on prices—you're betting on buying them from those who don't know how much they're worth and selling them to somebody who thinks they're worth more. That's speculation and it's short term. It's influenced and driven by supply and demand, and not by the worth of those companies whose value lies underneath that stock price."

—John Bogle

Founder and former CEO of the Vanguard Group
June 2009

"You can't invest your way to retirement. You've got to save your way to retirement."

—Gary Shilling

Economist
September 2009

Acknowledgments

FOR THE SAFE MONEY SYSTEM

An author's creativity and vision doesn't just happen. They are born out of a lifetime of success and failure, joy and sorrow, and victory and defeat. They are created with many "ties"—of love gained, lost and regained, of acceptance and rejection; and of the countess people and relationships that God brings across one's path in this life journey called Our Assignment.

I wish to express my sincere thanks and appreciation to all of those whom encouraged, challenged, and cheered me during my developmental years as an athlete and financial strategist.

To MY MOM AND DAD, thanks for never missing a game or an opportunity to encourage me that true success comes from giving your best effort, not winning or losing. I love you both for your unselfish participation in my life.

To MY LIFETIME FRIEND AND MY CATCHER FROM AGES 10-17, PASTOR GREG BERO, I have been blessed with your friendship and fellowship over these many years. Thanks for continuing to challenge me to remain humble and thankful during life's journey. And always remember that you stayed a catcher because I was a better pitcher!

To MY HIGH SCHOOL BASEBALL COACH, TONY GUGGIANA, I want to express thanks for teaching me that leadership, hard work, and humble appreciation for your teammates are far more important than wins and losses. I have tried to teach my sons that in life people will follow the person who leads by example, not simply words. Without your encouragement and discipline, I would never have had an eleven year professional career.

Acknowledgments

To my “other catcher” and soul-mate from my pro baseball days, Rick Bradley, I want to express thanks for knowing me thoroughly, and loving me in spite of it. Your friendship, prayers, and encouragement are fuel to my life.

To my core group of friends over the past twenty-five years: Thank you to Pastor Denny Bellesi, Phil Steffeck, Paul Ednoff, Buck Barbee, Scott Sterling and Mike Lococo for providing me a “safe place” to develop accountability and authenticity as a man, a father, a husband and a businessman. As Clarence the angel reminded George Bailey in *It's a Wonderful Life*: “Remember, no man is a failure who has friends.” God has truly blessed me with you all.

To my longtime friend and business associate, Vic Domines, I can't adequately express my thanks for your undying friendship, faith in my services for your clients, and your prayerful intercessions for my family, my business, and my life over these many years. You are a faithful warrior.

To my many clients from this thirty year endeavor, I wish to say thanks for your continual support, prayers, and referrals. Your trust and confidence in my services has provided our family a blessed lifestyle. Your understanding of my need to balance my time raising my boys and sharing their lives in sports and other activities has provided me the great memories of a dad who was able to “be there” for them.

To Michael Levin, I cannot adequately express my gratitude for your faithful contributions to make this book happen in a way that I never dreamed possible. Your talents, thoughtfulness and encouragement mean so much to me. God has given you a great gift of creativity, and the ability to bring it out in others. I am the grateful recipient of that gift.

To my mentor, Michael Gerber, I owe an incalculable measure of gratitude for your faith in my dream and vision to bless others by creating a financial system based on my experience and expertise. I can only shake my head in wonder at what you have drawn out of me through your excellent books, our Dreaming Room awakenings, and mentoring calls. This book is the direct result of your passion and lifelong calling to "awaken the entrepreneur within" me and others who are tired of just functioning adequately rather than extraordinarily. I look forward to the new awakenings that I know you will bring forth from me.

To David Yepiz, I want to thank you for your creativity and vision in developing the My Retirement Coach branding, and for all your hard work and energy during the formative stages of this journey.

To my sons, Nolan, Dillon and Dylan, I can only say that God has put greatness in all of you yet to be discovered and utilized for His purposes. Remember that greatness demands hard work, faithfulness, and gratitude to the One who bestowed His gifts and blessings on each of you. I'm proud to be your dad, and your friend. I love you!

To my son Brandon, I want to express my thanks and appreciation for trusting my mentorship and guidance as together we expand the vision that will arise from this book in creating a world-class company that will bless others and honor God. I love you, son. Thank you also to your wife Tiffany for her patient support and encouragement to our efforts.

What good is it to accomplish anything in this life that provides satisfaction and contentment without a great woman with whom to share it? To Crystal, my lover, friend, and wife, I want to thank you for your continual support, patience, and prayers during this often challenging journey in building the company of my dreams. Your beauty outside is the reflection of your beauty inside. A man is truly blessed when God gives him a "good woman," and you are truly that to me. I love you!

Foreword

By Michael Gerber

Internationally Best Selling Author of *The E-Myth*™ Books

It's shocking how badly we have been used by Wall Street.

It's shocking how deeply in debt we all really are, not just as individuals but as a society.

It's shocking how many poor investment decisions have been portrayed as "financial wisdom"—and now those same investment gurus are asking us to trust them again. It's like Lucy and the football. Well, it's time for investors like you to stop playing the role of Charlie Brown.

Read this book.

And then read it again.

Because the solution to your financial problem is discussed in thorough detail in this book. Randy Hammon has mastered that solution for you.

I first met Randy when he came to the Dreaming Room and we spent two and a half days together. I realized that here was an individual with the courage to stand up to Wall Street and the wisdom to share with investors about keeping their retirement money safe.

Best of all, it's not "rocket science."

It's not complicated.

It doesn't require you to put your financial life on the line once again.

All it calls for is a moral commitment to do the good work, an ethical forbearance to live the right way, and a solid, straightforward willingness to follow the simple path.

Hard to do?

I don't think so.

Americans have been doing that for generations.

What's hard to do is to repeat the same errors that brought us to where we find ourselves today, as a people, as a nation, as a society that finds itself suddenly economically upside down. When not that long ago, we were the cream of the universe, envied by all, copied by everyone, thought to be the leaders of the burgeoning new world.

How could so many supposedly smart people be so wrong?

Well, let's not take any more time thinking about it.

Let's get on with the book.

And Randy Hammon's brilliant solution to your financial future.

Contents

Part I

The ABCs of The Safe Money System

Chapter 1

Now What?

They stole your future

We all know who "they" are. Wall Street—the same people who told you, for all those years, that your money would be safe with them, that it would grow, and that if you played by the rules, you'd have all the money you needed when you needed it—for your children's education, for retirement, for that trip around the world.

You went on a trip, all right. Wall Street took you for a ride. That was your trip.

I'm not writing to you if you're a day trader, a gambler, a get-rich-quick kind of person, a penny stock lover, or someone who invests in every crazy scheme that comes on late-night infomercials. If those people lost everything, it really serves them right. That's not investing; that's gambling.

I'm not writing to the super wealthy whose lifestyle will not be affected if they lost 20 percent of their money in the Wall

Street Casino. Although, if the super wealthy aren't smart enough to control and secure the majority of their hard-earned money, I may be talking to them. There's nothing sadder than seeing wealth earned by the fruit of one's labor and expertise disappear in a risky endeavor outside one's expertise and control. And it happens all the time!

You're different. You've played by all the rules. You've worked hard all your life, scrimped and saved, lived on a budget, postponed gratification, and put money aside every month. Wall Street told you to put your money in stocks and stay in it for the long haul, and you followed the advice of the so-called experts. You did your homework. You picked the investments for your IRA, 401(k) or 403(b) plan, or other retirement plan that made the most sense in building your retirement nest egg. You allocated your assets, you weighed risks, and you thought you were taking the prudent course.

And look where it got you. Decades of investing and doing the right thing … wiped out in just a few horrible months. Now you don't even want to open your statements.

Your retirement ... gone.

Your savings ... decimated.

Your trust ... violated.

Your concerns and fears about the future … magnified beyond anything you could have imagined.

You were looking at retiring—maybe selling the house, taking the equity, and doing something you've always dreamed of. You fantasized about moving to Hawaii or some other dream location. Or maybe you'd just stay put, watch your grandchildren grow up, and help your kids from time to time with your money and time. Now your financial future has been shattered.

So the question arises: Now what? And that's the question this book seeks to answer. What do you do now? Whom do you trust? Where do you invest? How do you get made whole again? And how could this whole financial meltdown have happened in the first place?

Find Freedom from the Money Meltdown

I started off inside the Wall Street casino thirty years ago, so I know exactly what goes on there and how they put their interests ahead of yours. How they "pump and dump" stock on unsuspecting, trusting investors like you. How they make money whether you make it or lose it. I worked for one of the top brokerage firms for three years, and I was in the top 10 percent of producers at the firm. I made great money, especially for a young guy. I had the whole Newport Beach lifestyle—the fancy car, the house, the whole package.

I'll tell you my entire story a little later. But when it finally dawned on me how the Wall Street system was ripping off the very people we taught to trust us, I walked away. I walked away from a brokerage career that could have set me up for life in a few very short years. I didn't want any part of it. I saw how risky it was for you, the investor, and how much of a sure thing it was for the brokerage houses and Wall Street to win every time. Quite frankly, it made me sick to my stomach and mad as hell.

So I went a different direction. I went in the direction of creating safe investments—I call it Safe Money—for people who didn't have a gambling mentality and weren't looking for hot stock tips.

My primary clientele were schoolteachers, school administrators, law enforcement personnel, firefighters, and doctors and nurses who work in nonprofit hospitals—hard-working people who knew the value of a dollar and didn't make a fortune at their jobs but understood that if they invested wisely, they could have a secure future—and a lot less stress!

While everyone else was suffering from the market meltdown in 2008 and 2009, my clients never lost a dime in their retirement accounts or non-qualified personal accounts. In fact, over the last ten years, they've averaged returns of 7 percent annually.

Meanwhile, all the investors who didn't follow the Safe Money System you'll find outlined in this book took a licking in the market's collapse. Bit by bit, things are beginning to improve, and that's great. But the real question is: Has anybody learned from the mistakes of the last twenty years? Or are people just jumping back on the merry-go-round, only to be taken for a ride yet again?

If you want to learn how to grow your money safely, even in these turbulent, almost unprecedented economic times, I'll show you how to do so in this book. Wanna get rich quick? Hit on the next hot penny stock? Ride the wave of the latest easy money scheme somebody's peddling on an infomercial at 2 a.m.? Want me to compete with the financial network's talking heads, who didn't steer you to safety two years ago, even when they sensed things were heading over a cliff? Again, if you answered "yes" to any of those questions, then I'm not your guy.

If you desire to understand what really happened, why the key investment vehicles that Wall Street put you in were doomed to failure practically from the start, and above all what to do now, then come along for this journey. I'll give you a philosophy of investing and a strategy for going forward that Wall Street will never tell you about because if you've got Safe Money, they can't steal it from you. And that's what this book is all about.

Set Realistic Financial Goals

So how did we get in this mess in the first place?

When it comes to the way money changes hands between the individual investor and brokerage houses, I imagine Jack Nicholson delivering a line from Edward Winslow's book Blind Faith: "Well, the broker made money and the firm made money—and two out of three ain't bad."

Let's say an average investor—we'll call him Fred—sees a full-page ad in the newspaper about some innovative strategy of investing. He calls the number or visits the website to sign up and attends the seminar. What happens next? To paraphrase William Bernstein's writing in The Intelligent Asset Allocator, if Fred gains some knowledge and continues to do his own research and pick his own stocks, then he doesn't know that he doesn't know. What's Fred not grasping? He doesn't see how Wall Street makes money on his every move. Whether Fred's stock pick goes up, down, or sideways, the Wall Street casino cashes in.

What happens if Fred gives his money to a so-called "investment professional"? Now the money is in the hands of someone, in Bernstein's words, "who indeed knows that he or she doesn't know, but whose livelihood depends on them appearing to know." In other words, the financial advisors at Stocks 'R' Us know enough to get you to put money with them, but their knowledge about your investment choices is severely limited; they don't have complete access to the accuracy of the information received from their analysts. And what they don't know affects you. The consequences of their actions in peddling Wall Street's constant misinformation will leave you holding the bill. Fred, like the rest of us, is an innocent bystander who gave his money over to people who know little more than he does about investments! They know a lot about the process of selling you an investment, but they don't know much about the true worth of those investments, the risk level, and whether you should be buying them in the first place. So Fred, thinking he's about to take a walk down Easy Street, actually finds himself run over by an armored truck taking his money—and the money of all the other Freds of the world— to the Wall Street vault.

Finance gurus on CNBC, MSNBC, and other financial shows advised people to invest for the long run, implying that no matter how much money people lost today, they'd earn it back in the future. In January 1999, the S&P 500 Index read 1229; ten years later in 2009, it stood at 1000—an 18 percent decline. The numbers show that the S&P has not progressed much in the past decade. We might have another large drop ahead—we don't know. Somebody might have put their nest egg into the market a decade ago, only to see it drop as much as 40 to 50 percent at the bottom of the current market in early 2009.

At the same time, CDs, fixed annuities, and U.S. treasury bonds have proven secure—not sexy but secure. They grew at an average rate of 4 percent annually over the last ten years. People who held them are significantly ahead of those who did not. Ten years ago, an advisor would have said that investing in CDs, annuities, and treasury bonds was a stupid mistake. Today, a whole lot of people wish they had made that very mistake!

The strangest thing is that all this has happened before. After the crash of 1929, it took until 1954 for investors to get back to the breakeven level on the Dow-Jones Industrial Average. I know that sounds hard to believe, but it's true. If your grandfather lost his savings when the market crashed in October 1929, it would have taken him 25 full years before his investments returned to that level of the Dow.

If you don't believe me, look at the numbers. Numbers are your friend! The Dow peaked at 384 in late September 1929. A year later, in September 1930, it had slumped to 194, a 46 percent drop. By September 1931, in the bear market recovery (similar to the one we're experiencing today in 2009), it went back to 283—a 46 percent rebound. However, Grandpa was still down 26 percent from the market peak in September 1929. Then, in July 1932, the Dow crashed to 41 ... and that's not a typo! It went all the way down to 41. Even after a five-year gain of 385 percent between 1932 and 1937, the market only scratched back to 194, still 50 percent below the September 1929 high of 384.

Does this sound eerily similar to what's going on today? Just add a few zeroes to the Dow index number, and it's déjà vu all over again. The Dow peaked in October 2007 at 14,066. It dropped ... and dropped ... and dropped ... until it had reached 8,000 in October 2008—a 43 percent decrease. By March 2009, the Dow had dropped more to 6,440, a 54 percent plunge from its October 2007 peak, wiping out trillions of dollars of wealth—including, very possibly, much of your wealth.

As of this writing, in October 2009, the market was back to

9850. Terrific … but it's still thirty percent below the peak, even after a 50 percent rebound over the last six months.

Are you starting to see a similar historical pattern developing? If you want to know the future, look at the past. In the stock market, it's the 1930s all over again. Disaster, followed by government intervention and hype, followed by a false recovery based on nothing but wishful thinking and Wall Street hype, and followed by the reality check resulting in …

If you can't tell me what follows and you're betting your retirement future on that guess in the stock market, I would call you a gambler and your advisor a bookie! The bottom line is you can't afford to lose money. We'll get more deeply into this later on, but here's the first takeaway I want to share with you: A loss is much worse for you than a gain is good.

In light of the demonstrated history of losses, how is it that Wall Street keeps getting people to invest? By creating a false impression of security based on a false notion of expertise, that's how. If they can make you feel safe and that they absolutely know what they're talking about, you'll hand over your cash to them. That's the secret of their success.

As an investor, you must keep an especially sharp eye out for false impressions of security. One way to do that is to watch out when financial advisors start throwing out the names of celebrities or famous investors who own the stocks or investments they're pitching. Is there substance behind the pitch, or is it just another commercial or infomercial with a celebrity endorsement? A well-known name is often thrown out to increase the credentials of a risky investment. Such is the case when advisors say in order to get someone interested that Warren Buffett is buying this stock or Bill Gates is looking to acquire this company.

When I was a stockbroker, if I knew a big-name investor had a sizeable stake in a certain mutual fund or company I was pitching, you bet I would reference the name. The implication of my reference was simple: If the big guys are in on this stock, why aren't you? However, it's important to remember that the big guys may be wrong. After all, the net worth of Messrs. Buffett and Gates also decreased 30 percent in the latest stock market collapse! However, it wasn't their life savings.

There are consequences for not investigating the fundamentals behind mass fanfare for a stock. Back in the technology bubble from 1997 to 2000, some companies had zero earnings per share and no sales, but their stock was selling for $100 per share. Even an established company like Broadcom went from $9 in 1997 to over $170 at the top of the market in mid-2000. Then someone let the cat out of the bag: There was a total absence of real fundamentals. The value of Broadcom stock, and many other companies like it, was vastly inflated. People realized that the prices were based on a bubble created by Wall Street analysts who kept saying the stock was worth way more than it actually was. The analysts who said that the Broadcom stock was never going to stop growing saw that same stock go down from $170 to $125 in late 2000. But what did the stock brokerage salesman say? "If you liked it at $170, you've gotta love it at $125—buy more!"

Then the stock went down to $100 in early 2001. What did we hear from the broker? "Buy more!" When it went down to $50, he said, "You've got to be madly in love with it at $50." Subsequently, the stock went down all the way to $12 by late 2001, and nobody was buying it then, even at that low price. Investors were finally fed up with the continued misinformation from the bookies on Wall Street. You might as well have invested at a craps table at a Vegas hotel; at least that way, they might have given you a few free drinks or a shot at the buffet for your troubles.

In Dirty Harry, Clint Eastwood said, "A man has to know his limits." One of the basic rules of financial planning is to understand where you are in your life, not just where you would like to be. For example, at the end of his forty-year career, my father was making $55,000 a year climbing poles for Southern California Edison. He had three sons, and he had to face the facts: He wouldn't be able to send all three to the University of Southern California. He just couldn't afford a college fund—that would have jeopardized his ability to retire after risking his life on poles for forty years. That reality was one of my father's limits, which he and everyone else in our family recognized.

When people talk about limits today, there's often a negative connotation. But when I use the word limits, I don't mean it in a negative way. My definition of limit has to do with "comfort zone" or "what you can handle comfortably and effectively in life."

The reason people get scammed and make mistakes, such as choosing the wrong major in college or going after the wrong career, is that they fail to recognize their limits. Maybe they lacked someone in their lives who would help set parameters for them. In other words, no one sat down and helped them outline their beliefs, goals, passions, and limits—no one gave them that reality check, if you will.

Wall Street really likes to tell people to look at where they should be compared with other successful investors as if it were possible to obtain everything imaginable simply by playing a game of compare and contrast. This message is completely unrealistic; yet people keep buying into it. (Remember any of your friends bragging about Qualcomm at $740 a share? How many of them even knew what Qualcomm did? And how many of them were still bragging when the dot.com meltdown of 2001 occurred?)

The truth is that different skill levels and economic backgrounds create better opportunities and career choices for some people than for others, but a lot of people want to believe that all they have to do to change their fortune is dream big. I believe in big dreams … but in order to achieve them, you have to "wake up" from the nightmare created by Wall Street. It's time to start working on your dreams—not theirs!

That's why it's so important to keep an eye on your realistic limits. When a financial advisor comes along and tells you that he can make more money for you than what you are making right now, you have to ask realistic questions about what happens if he doesn't. When you walk into a Vegas casino, you should know how much you're willing, or how much you can afford, to lose. The same is true when you enter the Wall Street casino. You have to examine who you are, what you make, and what your goals are. Is it really possible to get an annual return of 10 to 20 percent on your investments over a ten to twenty-year period? The S&P 500 Index in the last fifty years brought average annual gains just under 7 percent. If you look at the Dow Jones, it also gained just under 7 percent. So how are any returns over 7 percent, as a financial advisor might claim that he can create for you, even remotely possible over the long haul given the history of investing you now know?

In my role as financial advisor, I often meet prospective clients who say, "My current broker is promising me annual returns of 10 percent. Can you match that?"

I tell them, "No, but I'll give you my best long shot in the fifth race at Santa Anita!" In all seriousness, I would be honest and give an answer based on reality. There's nothing real about getting 10 percent a year risk-free. The brokers may be getting great returns on your money—but you won't. The problem with many advisors is that they do not set parameters for their clients. They can't constantly put more and more money in the market and hope that the market will comply; they need to know when enough is enough. Investors don't need to know earnings per share; they need to know their own level of contentment. How much do you really need to be happy? Do you need all the money in the world? And are you willing to risk everything you already have to get that extra piece of the pie? Or do you have enough right now to live decently with enough in your investment portfolio so you can retire and live decently later on?

Investors need to remember that all objects of hope should be based on some sort of substantiated fact. That requires asking questions like the following: What is my current budget? How will I pay off college loans for my kids? Where do I want to live when I retire? How do I worry less about what is going to come later in life and enjoy life now so that when I get to my goals, my spouse is there with me instead of her divorce attorney? Parameters need to be set.

Avoid Financial Fallout

When betting on sports and on the floor of the New York Stock Exchange, knowledge is power. There's a huge imbalance of power in the financial markets. To put it simply, they have all the knowledge ... and all the power ... and you have none. They never tell you that.

Why should they?

Every time Fred, or anyone else, signs an agreement on the application to create a brokerage account, there's one sentence in the fine print that Fred doesn't notice and that his broker will never highlight. It's a disclaimer that can be summarized as follows: "We want to bring to your attention that there is a potential conflict of interest in our financial advice to you. We help raise money, do the initial public offerings, and underwrite for the very companies in which we are advising you to invest. We are going to try to not let this relationship sway us, but there is no guarantee."

Every single investor with every single brokerage house signs an application that contains a clause like this. Every single investor—all the Freds of the world—are unknowingly giving their stockbroker permission to allow a possible conflict of interest that could steal their future dreams.

So whose interest is most important to the brokerage house? Is it Fred's? Fred may have an account with $50,000, or even $500,000, in it. That's a lot of money to Fred, but it's a drop in the bucket compared to the fees and discounted stock prices that the brokerage houses receive from the companies they are pimping. (And I use that word intentionally, by the way.) Do you think they'll ever reveal to Fred any negative information about the companies whose stocks they are recommending? Of course not! That's because the broker-salesman doesn't know the entire story.

For a Wall Street brokerage house, the corporate finance entities typically come first, and the retail brokerage division comes second in fees generated and fortunes created for their executives. In essence, the executives of the brokerage houses and their corporate clients are reaping windfalls while the public is getting advice that is not always in its best financial interest. And guess who's left holding the bag?

Indeed, executives of major corporations are making incredibly large sums of money that you never hear about. Maybe you're old enough to remember the early 1980s when Chrysler was on the verge of bankruptcy, and the company stock was down to just $3 per share. The head of Chrysler at the time, Lee Iacocca, went to Congress and basically said: "Give us a billion dollars in loan guarantees so that we can function, or I'm going to bankrupt the company and you will have to pay $1.5 billion for our pension plan." So Congress made what seemed like the prudent decision at the time and bailed out Chrysler for $1 billion.

I know Iacocca is considered one of the great American financial heroes, but unfortunately, there's more to the story. He didn't just save jobs—he made himself a fortune. Iacocca accepted a salary, after the government bailout, of $1 per year. But Iacocca also owned stock options as the top Chrysler executive, probably in the $3 to $5 per share range. After the bailout—after taxpayers footed the bill for Chrysler's recovery—the price of Chrysler's stock soared to $48 a share within seven years. Iacocca made millions and millions of dollars by exercising his stock options, a fact that the American people never knew about. Did taxpayers share in that windfall? Of course not! Iacocca was a hero, all right—to his accountant, his family, and his estate.

Ever since, CEOs have looked at the Iacocca story and asked one simple question: "Where's mine?" And the pay of top executives has skyrocketed ever since to levels that are truly obscene. I don't mind seeing people being highly compensated for a job well done. But do these guys really deserve hundreds of millions of dollars—even as they drive their companies into the ground? I certainly don't think so. And guess who's paying for all that salary?

Look in the mirror, Mr. or Ms. Taxpayer.

They get rich because of your willingness to trust them with your money, and they don't even send you thank you notes. Imagine how cramped their hands would get having to write to millions of Freds all over the country—indeed, all over the world—thanking you for your tax contributions to their astonishing wealth.

The story of Lee Iacocca and the Chrysler bailout is relevant today more than ever. Newly hired executives have been approved by the government to run banks and Wall Street firms that are just coming out of bankruptcy due to the economic collapse of 2008 and 2009. Fearing public outrage, the compensation of these new executives is closely monitored for excess. While these executives are forbidden to get large salaries and bonuses, it does seem to be more acceptable for them to participate in stock options, if they perform well with taxpayer funds. Believe me—their employers will have no problem skirting regulations and paying them the big bucks.

The executives own company stock as part of their compensation, and they are able to get stock options while the prices are very low. However, the public doesn't know when and how the executives are going to get extra money because the ones at the top have access to information that you don't. They know just when to pull the trigger on their stock options because they know when bad news is coming that will depress the price of the stock. It's legalized insider trading. And the average investors—the Freds of the world—are stuck at the wrong end of the un-level playing field. When you buy a stock (from those in the know), you're guessing. When they sell a stock (to you), they're acting out of solid knowledge that you don't have.

Unless you know what's going on inside the Wall Street firms, it's next to impossible to make as much money as the executives make. The people who make the most money betting the horses are those who got a tip from a jockey or a trainer. By analogy, the people who do well on Wall Street have access to information that the rest of the public does not have. The executives of the corporations and brokerage houses make all the money. The public receives a small piece of the pie after all the management, administrative, and other fees they charge.

There's a perception that the executives of the bailed-out institutions are being paid low salaries, but the public has no idea to what extent these seeming "heroes" are excessively compensated with stock options. If the public knew, there would be more outrage than the executives could handle. So, naturally, the public will never know.

Something else I find outrageous is the way the market still tells the average Joe that he can make millions overnight just by investing his life savings in the market. There's an ongoing bombardment of such propaganda as if the market meltdown had never happened. How dumb do they really think we are? For example, you might remember an ad featuring a taxi driver who is also a successful day trader; he only drives a taxi because he owns the taxi company. Then there was the ad showing a wine connoisseur who invested her money in a 401(k) and somehow made enough to buy her own vineyard. The only way she could have made that kind of money would be if she'd invested with Bernie Madoff … and somehow got out before he went bust.

As a result of those ads, people often begin to think that investing is always glamorous and lucrative, and they don't think about the risks involved. The message is always, "Look how easy it is to be a stock trader! Even your grocer is making a fortune." The same appeal to greed attracts people to Las Vegas with the same results: You'll always hear the boasts about how much people made, but people never tell the truth about how much money they lost.

People like to feel important, and that sense of self-importance is fueled by their ability to say "my advisor" or "my attorney" or "my broker." So even when their broker is losing money, they'll still praise him and say something like, "He promises me that I'll recover my losses by making me more than 10 percent a year going forward." Wall Street is trying to provide an environment where people think that easy money can be made no matter the circumstance. They'll do anything to perpetuate the idea that such a place actually exists, until all the people they've conned are practically lying in the gutter, dead broke.

It was no different in real estate. Anyone who has worked in real estate or has owned a house knows that approximately every ten or twelve years, we cycle between bull and bear markets, meaning there's always a chance that house prices will fall. Yet, due to the fear of missing out on the market or the desire to make more money, people refinanced their houses and threw their equity into either the over-priced stock market or into overinflated real estate. Then they refinanced their houses again or sold them in an attempt to make more money with another stock or real estate strategy.

But, as we all know, trees don't grow to the sky. After a decade or so of easy money, some people lost everything they made earlier. How? By buying a house at the top of the market with easy financing from the banks before the downturn came. Now, after the housing market has collapsed, some can't refinance the house they have and some can't buy the same house they sold a decade ago under the new, higher qualification standards. Others can't tap the equity in their homes because banks won't qualify them for home equity lines of credit. Only in retrospect, people ask, "Why didn't anyone point out that there was a major possibility the real estate market would go bust after seeing house prices triple in the past ten years?"

It's a great question. Why didn't anybody try to stop the music? None of the talking heads on MSNBC or CNBC stepped up to say, "Now is the time to be safe and get out of the market" or "It's time to stop playing the real estate game in the midst of a bubble." Why? Because these networks are funded by Wall Street firms. Who advertises on them? The Wall Street investment houses. It's a simple case of "whose bread I eat, his song I sing." So much for "impartial" investment advisors. On these networks, the on-air "talents" do nothing more than promote themselves, their services, books, and magazines, or whatever else they have to offer. No one sells anything in a bull market by telling people to get out of the market. And no one wants to hear negative news that would hurt their investment portfolios.

Nobody paid attention to the fact that from 2005 to 2007, many people who couldn't have qualified in the past under prudent underwriting standards were suddenly able to buy a half-million dollar house in a heartbeat with nothing more than a pulse and a false Social Security number. The banks allowed these purchases, and the executives on Wall Street demanded them. Everybody knew. The job of a mortgage portfolio professional in a bank is to package those loans, get them to Wall Street, let others peddle them off to somebody else, and continue the process. Yet no one spoke out about the outrageous activities they witnessed in the markets because they would have lost their jobs. The media "covering" Wall Street was really just covering up for Wall Street. Fear and greed ruled once again—the old familiar culprits.

Some people have finally gotten fed up. One of the bestselling financial gurus who for years championed the strategy of the "little guy" investing in stocks has now become a spokeswoman for the FDIC, an organization charged with guaranteeing bank safety. But before her involvement with the FDIC, this woman told investors to stay in the market for the long run no matter what or they wouldn't be able to retire. My response to her is simply to pick one side or the other. It's a choice between gambling and safety. And only now are you telling all those millions of "little guys" you advised to gamble their hard-earned dollars on the stock market to aim for safety and security. Thanks a lot!

The truth is that Wall Street was never on your side, even when it was making a fortune off of you. What's mindboggling for me is the fact that many Wall Street firms do not offer adequate downside protection plans for their clients. When I was a stockbroker, I learned about a strategy that the wealthy clients had used for years:

If you had a lot of money in the market, you always employed stock protection options. For example, you would pay the option premium of a strategy that allowed your broker to sell your stocks if the prices fell below a certain level. As a result, you wouldn't lose beyond 12 to 15 percent of your investments. Why weren't Mom-and-Pop investors—the little guys—offered this same protection? Probably because their brokers never wanted to raise the ugly possibility that stocks could go down.

Over and over again, we've witnessed the irresponsibility that corporate executives display toward shareholders, the public, and regulators. The executives must think that they are above the law because they've gotten away with rubbing financial excess in the public's face for so long. At least most bank and insurance companies that received taxpayer bailout money in 2008 and 2009 had the foresight to cancel their award trips for their top producers and executives. But more visible limits on corporate excess must be put in place to gain back the public's trust. What does trust and integrity mean when we see AIG insurance executives spending thousands of taxpayer dollars partying away at the St. Regis Resort in California? What triggered the party? Why the news of AIG's bailout with hundreds of billions of dollars of taxpayer money!

We also have the example of GM and Chrysler executives flying separately in their private jets to plead poverty before Congress when their corporations were on the verge of bankruptcy. How do we define trust when Bernard Madoff, the financier who people and institutions in the top ranks of our society trusted, cheated his investors out of tens of billions of dollars? The SEC was repeatedly tipped that there were major issues with Madoff concerning his investment strategies ... but why wasn't a thorough investigation performed?

The reason might have been that there is indeed a good-old-boy network operating on Wall Street. After all, Madoff had a solid reputation as the former chairman of Nasdaq, which meant that he'd had past dealings with the regulatory agencies of Wall Street. It's no wonder people fell over themselves to invest with Madoff even though insiders on Wall Street and in the government had solid information that he was running a massive scam ... and that he had been doing so for years. How else was it possible for him to show 15 percent annual gains at times when the market was down as much as 40 percent? But you didn't have to be a friend of Bernie's to get burned. All you had to have was a few extra dollars in your bank account...and a dream.

If we want to dig ourselves out of the ditch we're in and ensure that something like this doesn't happen again, then we need to stop giving over our financial futures to a system based on imperfect knowledge. The brokerage house knows all but doesn't tell all; the investor knows little but hopes for the best. It's like Lucy pulling the football away from Charlie Brown. You'd think that kid would wise up after a while. He doesn't, and as investors, neither do we.

One of my friends often tells me, "I don't want to open the statement from my broker. I don't want to know. My broker told me not to stress out and that the money is going to come back in the long run. I'm not worried." Then my friend always turns to me and asks, "Are you worried?"

I am worried! Yes, I am. I am worried about investors not knowing what to do next. I know that deep down my friend is worried too. In order to eliminate the stress, we need to understand the fundamental principles of investing for ourselves, so that we can start controlling our own assets. Our money can only be considered Safe Money if we know where it is today and where it will be tomorrow. In this book, I want to show you how to keep your money safe.

We as investors have abdicated our responsibility for our finances to others who might not know the basic concepts necessary to do what is best with those finances. The basic concepts are knowledge, understanding, and control. These concepts are not applied by investors because they don't know, don't understand, or don't control what's going on with their finances. Furthermore, we don't tend to treat our advisors as partners when we should do so. One of the reasons might be intimidation: We're afraid to tell the professionals what to do because we hire them to tell us what to do. We say, "Here is the money and I trust you." Things should not be that way. We need to pick our advisors based on how they have protected their clients over the last ten to twenty years ... instead of letting them have free reign over our money in the Wall Street casino.

In this book, I would like to assist you with your finances by helping you set proper parameters for your financial life. Anyone can develop his or her own strategy of how to handle money by understanding their own core values and what is important to them. A solid future sits on a three-legged stool: finances, relationships, and your health. Take out any one of those legs and the stool will collapse. Your relationships and your health are your business. Your financial success is my responsibility.

I want you to develop a customized strategy unique to your goals and your hopes rather than overloading you with information that does nothing but paralyze your decision-making process. Knowledge is not the issue here. Today thanks to the information explosion on the Internet, you as a solo investor have more tools to gain knowledge about investments than I had at my disposal as a stockbroker 25 years ago. It's all about how you use it.

Anyone can follow my advice, no matter his or her socioeconomic background. Whether you or your parents went to Yale or jail, this approach will work for you. My dream for you is that you be content, no matter what your current situation. If you can learn to be content with where you are at this time in your life, your finances, your relationships, and your health will do nothing but flourish. Whether you work for the government, in education, law enforcement, the medical field, or in the private sector, I can help you. Together, we'll figure out an answer to that puzzling question, "Now what?"

In order to do so, I'd like to take a step back in time and tell you a little about how I came to develop the Safe Money System™ in the first place, and that's the topic of the next chapter.

Chapter 2

Losing My Wall Street Virginity

When I grew up in the 1950s and '60s, inflation was low, mortgage interest rates were low, and people lived within their means. You didn't have large unsecured credit debt—if you missed a payment on the TV or an appliance, the store would come repossess it. Banks underwrote home loans based on (imagine this) your ability to pay it back, which they calculated from real income and real assets. Because of prudent credit underwriting and without easy money thrown into the economy by the Fed, housing values didn't grow beyond the average worker's grasp.

I remember that my family struggled with money when I was a kid. None of my relatives on either side of the family ever went to college, owned a business, or belonged to a country club. My dad worked his behind off and risked his life for 35 years climbing utility poles in high winds, heavy rains, and blistering heat in

Southern California—but he was never going to make or save a lot of money as a lineman for Southern California Edison.

My mom handled the money and the bills in our family. That meant trying to take Dad's paycheck and figure out each month how to meet all the bills. My two brothers and I always seemed to have plenty to eat, nice clothes, the best sports equipment, and we took an annual vacation for a week to the mountains or Catalina Island. But looking back, we were a lower middle-class family from Gardena, California, a suburb of Los Angeles.

The critically important factor is this—we were always content with what we had, who we were, and how we lived. We didn't compete with the neighbors concerning cars, home amenities, or wealth. Nor did I ever hear my parents complain that they lacked material things, exotic vacations, or a bigger home. They bought a bigger home when they could afford it as Dad's income gradually increased with seniority. Only then did we get a better car and take better vacations. All of us boys could go to private Catholic grammar and high school. A night on the town for dinner usually meant a visit to an upscale coffee shop.

My mom didn't have to work in order for us to afford a decent, comfortable lifestyle. So she stayed at home and raised the kids, and we kids knew we were safe and secure for the most part. Yeah, the "stop and drop" drills in the early 60s were a little unnerving—practicing ducking under your desk to avoid a nuclear bomb. But they weren't nearly as unnerving as growing up in a single-parent home where your mom is forced to work to support herself and her kids or being raised by a string of unknown nannies. In retrospect, it was far better to have only one income from my dad and to have my mom home with us in a smaller house than to be raised in a McMansion by the nanny with both parents having to work to support the lifestyle.

My maternal grandmother lived in nearby Inglewood and demonstrated to me how to create wealth with real estate. She owned four pieces of property, she never worked, and my grandfather was a low-level aerospace worker. But she was a saver, and when she invested, she controlled the investment—not some Wall Street bookie. She always told me stocks were for "rich folks"—I think she meant people who could afford to lose money on stock investments without it affecting their lifestyles. Growing up in the Great Depression really made simple folk like my grandmother very wise. "Don't live beyond your means." "Don't buy something you can't afford." "Control your investments in safe savings or by buying real estate." Seems like sound advice, I think you'll agree!

Back in 1948, Grandma bought a small house in Newport Beach, 50 yards from the sand for just $18,000. Today, the house is worth over $2,000,000, and it's condition is barely better than it was 60 years ago! While my grandma always fretted about money in discussions with Mom, she always seemed to have cash to loan to my folks toward their next down payment. The crucial point is that money was always a loan, never a gift—yet another great lesson I learned from grandma on teaching your kids responsibility rather than enablement.

And what did I learn about banking as a kid from my grandma? I learned that if you put your money in several bank accounts, you get a lot of free stuff: toasters, calendars, record albums, and ballpoint pens. I learned this because that's what my frugal grandma would give us kids for Christmas and birthdays!

I grew up never expecting to be rich or truly happy—only that you pursue both but attain neither. I knew I didn't want to climb utility poles in rainstorms and high winds like my dad. I wanted to wear suits not Levi's. The lesson for students in the mid-1960s was that we had better go to college to stay out of Vietnam along with the additional motivation of getting a better job and lifestyle than our parents had.

Fortunately, God gave me a wonderful talent that turned out to be my ticket to an exciting life, the fruits of which I continue to enjoy today. I could throw a baseball hard and far (in addition to a football). I couldn't run a lick, and my jumping ability was limited to touching the doorframe inside our home—but I had one helluva right arm. And from age ten to fifteen, I was an All Star pitcher on every baseball team I played on—the best travel teams in Southern California.

Upon graduation after a successful senior year, the Kansas City Royals drafted me in the 1969 pro baseball amateur draft. I had several full scholarship offers to great private colleges, so I told the Royals that I was going to college as my father had always encouraged me to do. He had pitched for a year in low minor-league ball in the late 1940s and always advised me that an education was more important than sports in the end.

I was very fortunate that my parents always helped me set boundaries regarding the choices I made, choices that would lead me towards fulfilling my goals for the future. After I rejected several offers that were outside of those boundaries, Kansas City gave me nearly as much money as their top draft pick in order to keep me. But I only signed with them if they included a very unusual clause in my contract—that I could complete my college education and just play during the summers until I was twenty-one (I graduated high school at not yet seventeen-and-a-half). Moreover, they couldn't release me from my contract during that time. I have never heard of such a contract before or since—but I knew my limits. I knew what was best for me, and I was willing to walk away from the money if the Royals didn't consider my boundaries acceptable to them.

While I played professional baseball, I also managed to go to Loyola University of Los Angeles. For the first two years of my career, I attended school full time and worked out with the college team. During my third season, I played baseball for half the year and went to school for the other half. I took on a lot of academic responsibility during my first six minor-league years in the off-season, usually taking over fifteen units in Business Administration, working out starting in January with Loyola's team, and working a part-time job.

By age twenty, I was one of the top starting pitcher prospects in the Kansas City Royals organization. I was flown from my Single-A team in June 1972 to Pittsburgh to see what I could do against the world champion Pittsburgh Pirates at Three Rivers Stadium in an exhibition game in front of 40,000 fans. I threw no-hit ball for three innings in relief. Then in 1973 at age twenty-one, I led the Double-A Southern League with a 2.13 ERA for about 180 innings. At age twenty-two, I finally got a Big League contract with Kansas City for 1974 and 1975 and pitched in Triple-A for them. From 1976 to 1980, I went on to play with the New York Mets and San Francisco Giants Triple-A teams and did very well. The Mets flew me into Cooperstown, New York to pitch in the 1976 Hall of Fame exhibition game against the Milwaukee Brewers. What a great thrill!

Then came misery. I suffered a shoulder injury when I slipped on a wet mound during a rainstorm in my third game in the Puerto Rican Winter League after the 1978 season, and it never healed sufficiently over the winter. After being invited to the Giant's major league camp but being unable to perform at my peak level and enduring a frustrating 1979 season with the Triple-A Giants in Phoenix, I left the game I so loved.

I never had surgery, and my shoulder healed on its own within a year of my retirement at age 28. Back in 1979, there were neither arthroscopic surgeries nor MRIs, and any exploratory surgery would have ended my career anyway. To this day, my arm is still strong, and I never needed an operation.

The Giants asked me to train to become a manager in their organization, but again, that choice would have been outside the boundaries I set for my life after baseball. I wanted to be in control of where I lived—where I worked—and to have some semblance of control over my long-term job security. So I moved on. My eleven-year baseball career had been good, not spectacular, but it was highly satisfying to be able to live my dream of playing professional ball and to get a great education. But the journey came to an end, and I found myself asking the same question with which we started this book:

Now what?

No one in my family was a finance guru, so I was pretty much on my own when it came to understanding personal finance. When I signed my baseball contract coming out of high school, I didn't even know how to balance a checkbook. Because no one in my family had been in higher education, I didn't know what classes to take in college. I ended up being a business major because of my dad who told me, "Well, take business because anybody can do anything with a business degree." I wasn't sure how my dad knew that, but I followed his advice. I also went on to work on my MBA degree at Loyola while I was still playing ball.

To be honest, I wasn't fond of the course material for the business degree. It was boring because it's all about how to work for a major corporation and use business models on management theory. The degree had nothing to do with entrepreneurship, capital development, or investment banking. As a result of my dissatisfaction, I wasn't sure what I wanted to do for a living when I finished college and got out of baseball. By pure chance, I dropped my résumé by a headhunter's office in Newport Beach, California; one of the recruiters asked me if I'd ever considered being a stockbroker. She said her dad enjoyed the profession as it afforded him a good lifestyle and flexible hours in the afternoons.

I told the truth. I said no, I had never thought of being a stockbroker. To me, a stockbroker was a high-powered position because it involved dealing with people's money. It meant a nice office building and three-piece suits. It was a big deal. I never imagined myself working as an investment manager or financial advisor because I didn't know anyone who had ever done it. I talked to a few guys back in the 1970s who wanted me to invest my baseball bonus money in the stock market. But I just put my bonus money in the bank and never lost it. I played it safe because I needed the money for graduate school or maybe a down payment on my first house. I ended up using it for both.

The recruiter arranged for an interview for a stockbroker position at Kidder, Peabody & Co., a traditional Wall Street firm based on the East Coast. The firm had a great reputation and high standards. It also had a branch division in Newport Beach, California. Everything about Kidder said "Money and Wealth." I went into my first job interview in a three-piece, light-peach polyester suit. That wasn't a misprint—it was a peach-colored suit! Since my baseball career had called for a very casual wardrobe, it was the only suit I owned, but it would have made John Travolta proud! I don't think you could even find a peach suit on eBay today!

The interviewer didn't ask me much about stocks and investing. To him, it mattered that I was personable and had pretty good conversational skills. He seemed impressed that an ex-jock like me could read a book that didn't have pictures! Most importantly, he needed a good softball player for their broker league team, so who could have been a better recruit? That's how I began my career in Wall Street.

Starting out in the job as a stockbroker in 1980, I had no idea what the purpose of the Federal Reserve was or what the impact of mortgage interest rates was on the economy. As part of the training program, I had to get to the office at 5:30 in the morning to pour coffee for people because I was the rookie. Nonetheless, from Kidder's national training class that spring, I became the number-one producer out of a class of 65 people for my first full year of business production. I was only 28 years old at the time and made triple the income I'd made in my last year in pro baseball.

When I got my securities license and began learning what it meant to be a financial advisor, I discovered a problem: As a financial advisor, you are really a salesman. At 28 years of age, I was not cut out to be an advisor to anybody. What was I going to tell a 57-year-old multi-millionaire about money? I didn't know anything about money! I couldn't relate to a business owner or someone with huge inherited wealth. All I knew was that when my firm handed me an analyst report on the tech, oil, healthcare, or construction industry, it was my job to regurgitate the info and sell the stock or investment to my clients.

My manager would give me a phonebook or a stack of lead cards and say, "Call these people up and ask them if they are in the market. If they are, ask them if they would like a free report on a particular sector of the market from Kidder, Peabody."

People would say yes to the free report because they wanted to get me off the phone. I would send the report with my business card and say that I would call back in a week to ask, "What do ya think?" I knew that half the time, the people I called read little or none of the material I sent them. But I would follow up and say "If you are in the market, why don't you try this with some of your money?" This was my understanding of financial planning back then.

I didn't know anything about estate planning, tax consequences, or retirement planning—the tools that presently confirm my expertise as a financial strategist with thirty years of experience. After so many years, it is obvious to me that when it comes to personal finance, understanding how taxes affect your investment strategy and providing your clients with a lifetime income plan is much more important than reading from an analyst report about a certain industry you really know nothing about.

Learning Lessons the Hard Way

In 1981, oil was at $10 a barrel, and then it jumped to $42 a barrel in just eight months. The expectation was that oil prices would continue going up because of tensions in the Middle East, and that excited everyone. People picked energy stocks with their emotions, but they might as well have picked a stock by throwing darts at a dartboard. In fact, back then the Wall Street Journal had an entertaining feature in which stock "experts" would pick stocks against a monkey. More often than not, the monkey won!

Back then, the oil stocks just sharply increased, business was booming, and I was getting referrals left and right. I thought I was pretty smart. My clients quadrupled their money in six months as we used leverage by borrowing on the gains to invest in more energy stocks. During that time, I bought my first house and leased a new Mercedes.

As it turns out, six months later, I couldn't afford my new house or car anymore. The majority of the energy service, production, and development companies went bankrupt and everything collapsed. I realized that I wasn't so smart after all—and unfortunately, many of my clients learned the same thing the hard way.

Before the stock market bust of the early 1980s, people thought I was knowledgeable and wise. But I was just a salesman who could talk a good game and who happened to sell the right product at the right time. Everybody lost money on the stocks I promoted. When the collapse happened, it hurt, particularly because nobody at the firm told me that people could lose it all so quickly. Some people at the firm even got mad at me for selling the remaining toxic stocks in some of my clients' portfolios so as to at least preserve something.

I sold in spite of my firm's research department's "hold" recommendations because one of my clients had advised me of a thing or two: He told me that when circumstances are bad, people sell no matter what, and they would sell everything. He said to me, "Randy, I'd get out. I'd get all your clients out." He was the first guy who exposed me to the fear and greed that drives the financial markets. And he was right. Most people that I worked with still had some money after I sold.

The truth is, even when the market seemed stable and profitable, the public was not making as much money as they expected. After inflation, taxes, and management fees and commissions, people were lucky to receive 60 percent of their annual gross gains, and much less, of course, when there were losses!

I realized that I am a people person, and my idea of doing business did not align with the way 90 percent of Wall Street did business at the time. Most of the time at work, I had to have a phone stuck in my ear. Of all the people I opened new accounts for, I never met 75 to 80 percent of them in person.

Moreover, I realized that I was just gambling with stocks at Kidder, Peabody. I had had enough. In early 1982, I switched firms. I received a one-year guarantee for a higher salary to move my accounts to the new firm. Yet the stock market tanked to levels not seen since the 1930s (adjusted for inflation). Fed up with the whole Casino game mentality on Wall Street, I only stayed at the new investment firm for three months. I told my new manager that my heart wasn't in it. I didn't have any passion for it at all. I gave up the guaranteed income for the next nine months during the worst recession since the 1930s. He lost a good softball player for his team as well.

I hated losing people's money and being wrong. I hated sitting down with a guy like Fred—a man with a family, an account filled with his life savings, and a plan for retirement—and telling him that the analysts were saying that this was going to happen, yet knowing that it may or may not happen. It was like telling Fred, "I don't know what I'm talking about, but would you give me your money?" If I lost Fred's savings, how would I explain the failure? Nobody could really explain it to me. People would usually say, "Just stay in the market and things will come back," or "Buy more stocks when the price is lower." That was always their answer, but it wasn't good enough for me.

I did however remember one overriding thought as I examined the whole Wall Street scene. Investing is a 50/50 proposition: You either win or lose. So why was it that 80 percent of the time the firm's analysts told you to buy or hold? Shouldn't they be telling you to sell as often as they told you to buy? They didn't want to issue sell recommendations because they didn't want to upset the corporations with whom they had investment banking relationships! Over the long haul, it was more like "Heads I win, tails you lose" ... even though Wall Street is always telling people to invest for the long haul.

I also recognized that I was a salesman selling an intangible. There were too many moving parts to this intangible product that I didn't understand. I didn't know what was going on behind the scenes to create the financial products that I was selling. I knew money was made with inside information that the public didn't have. Everyone in this business knows that. Yet, using inside information is illegal, so how was it possible for my clients to make a boatload of money legally? The logic didn't add up and neither did my clients' results.

I didn't like what I was doing in financial planning even though I was successful. In my first full year of production, out of forty-five people in the office, I was number five. So when I left the world of big-time, blue chip investment firms, I wasn't running from failure by any means. I just couldn't bring myself to sell someone a product that not only didn't make them much money but might also kill their savings.

The Birth of the Safe Money System™

I wanted another career direction. I wanted to help people who didn't want to risk their hard-earned money in the Wall Street casino. I wanted their money to be safe. And I found such a business by working with educators.

To teachers, there was no such thing as financial planning. Most teachers—just like most people who work for companies (middle managers and down)—are average people. They make a good living and have good benefits. But they are not candidates to pay $2,000 to $5,000 for somebody to create a financial plan for them and sell them life insurance. It doesn't make sense for teachers to do that. If they sought me out, I could take a yellow legal pad and in one page plot out their finances. I would tell them, "You've got this amount of money; you need to put it here. Tell me when you want to retire, and I will tell you what you need to do to get to your goals." That's it.

Yes, teachers also need life insurance. Well, guess what? They have group benefits—health and life insurance—because they work in education. They also have very little chance of being fired or relocated. Most financial planners make a large percentage of their income not from giving advice but from selling insurance. If a client can buy insurance at a better rate than the financial planner can provide, where's the incentive for a financial planner to work for someone like a teacher?

We can give teachers tax advice. I can get a calculator out and look at the tax savings on what they put away in their supplemental pension fund. If Fred's wife Janet, a schoolteacher, puts away $100 worth of credit in this fund, it would only cost her $70 because of her tax savings. That's a pretty good deal. How much Janet could afford to put away was based on her monthly bottom-line budget. What I do as a financial strategist is all about teaching people who aren't skilled in taxes and financial calculations how to take control of their finances.

When I finally got around to the teacher market, I was very good at it. I didn't work for anyone; I was independent. I would do seminars, go to teachers' unions, and tell the teachers, "I don't want an endorsement from you. I know a lot of companies are looking for endorsements. I just want to do tax and retirement workshops." From 1988 to 1992, I built my business with just that routine. During my 30-year career in this business, I've always been in the top 1 percent in production for every insurance or financial services company I've ever represented, including Metlife, Allianz Life, Aviva USA Life, Old Mutual, and Great American Life.

This is how my Safe Money System™ began to come into existence. One of the most important aspects of the Safe Money System™ that I created was to make sure the investment strategies that I offered my clients were as safe as they could be, so that when a downturn like the recent one rolled around, my clients could keep their heads above water.

In the last decade, the insurance industry created a product that allows people to participate in stock market gains but not losses. Basically, the product consists of an "indexing strategy," which has a lock-in mechanism to prevent losses in its clients' accounts. The insurance companies would buy options in the indexes and invite people to put money in and participate. They would give these participants a percentage of the gains per year and keep a percentage. To me, that's a great deal, and I let my clients in on it.

The indexing strategy gets right in line with my record of helping my clients make 7 percent year after year for the last fifteen years, since the indexes also offered 7 percent gains on someone's investment. I figured that no one would lose a dime with the indexing strategy. Even if the market collapsed, and other people lost 50 percent of their principal in some mutual fund, my clients with the indexing strategy would still have what they had. Going into the next year, my clients might make zero if conditions are bad, but they would not lose money.

Here's the bottom line: As a ballplayer turned stockbroker, I discovered just how dangerous the Wall Street casino was for those who entered it. Along the way, I developed a system for helping regular folks keep their money safe—the Safe Money System™. No losses in the bad years. No exposure to risk. Safe, controlled growth. It turned out that the Safe Money System™ was working and working really well. I couldn't have been more pleased…and my clients felt the same way.

That's how the Safe Money approach came to be. The fable of the tortoise and the hare is relevant to a lesson I want to share about Safe Money. People might ask my clients, "Why are you making 7 to 8 percent when you can make 20 to 30 percent like the markets did in 1998 and 1999 or in 2004?" I would respond that what's important is not how fast you're earning at any one given point during the race (the competition of seeing whose stock portfolio gains the most over the short term). But rather it's more important what happens when you need to cash your chips in and create a retirement solution that guarantees you and your family security for the rest of your life. In other words, it doesn't matter if you are making 10 or 20 percent one year and losing 30 or 40 percent the next year. What matters is what you have in the end.

Sure, it doesn't feel good when a cousin or a co-worker's gain on their portfolio beats your gain by a couple of percentage points. But remember, his portfolio most likely involves more risk, which means that he has a greater chance of losing what he made all along. In the end, you will be glad to have more money to retire on because you played it safe. You were wise enough not to take seriously those cocktail party interrogations of why your investment gains fell short a few percentage points compared to the next guy.

The bottom line is that you do not want to be in this situation: Your broker told you to throw your money into the stock market for the long run. He promised that you would make 10 to 15 percent gains from when you are fifty-five to sixty-five years old. Now sixty-five is here, but all of a sudden, something like what happened in late 2007 to mid-2009 hits your investments; you look up and more than half of your money in the market is gone. To add to the problems, you are now "retired" and jobless. Your old job has either disappeared or gone offshore, or they've hired a twenty-something at a third of your salary to perform the work. Doesn't this situation sound absolutely terrible? I want to help you avoid it.

The difference between most Wall Street stockbrokers and me is that they are encouraged by their firms to peddle products that have a higher risk level than I feel most Americans can tolerate for their core retirement savings. So, since 1983, I've chosen not to sell any investments that have any risk of principal for my client's qualified retirement accounts. It has proven to be a great strategy for keeping clients! Here's why: In every deal I've ever seen created in Wall Street, whether it was a limited partnership in real estate or something to do with oil and gas, the general partners behind these deals always made their money before the average passive investor. Investing in anything risky is the same as playing poker with a bunch of strangers. As the old adage goes, if you look around the table and can't figure out who the patsy is, it must be you. So I always made sure that my clients, the "average investors" of the world, did not get taken advantage of by the wheelers and dealers.

For example, back in the late 1980s and early 1990s, Prudential created a bunch of partnerships in oil and gas and real estate that just flat-out failed. The company even was severely fined, and many of the executives of those brokerage divisions were indicted for what they had allowed to happen. The limited partnerships in Wall Street slowly grew less popular because a lot of money was lost in these deals.

The majority of guys in the financial planning industry played with fire and lived on the edge with high-risk products over the last twenty years. As a result, they have lost their credibility and most of their client base. Those investors are disillusioned. They are sour and perplexed as to how they continue to be their firm's fools to keep pimping these losing investments. I hope that many of those frustrated advisors are reading this book, so they can learn how to create Safe Money strategies for their clients—and their families as well.

A Gambler's Game

When a client comes to me, gives me $100,000, and asks me to manage it, I'm going to ask them a lot of questions like the following:

"What do you want to accomplish with this money?"

"What is this money for?"

"How much more money do you have?"

"If this is your retirement money, can you afford to lose it?"

Before you jump into any kind of investment, it is important to think about how your life is going to be affected if you were to lose the money you invested. For example, I bet on the tech industry in the late 1990s and lost every dime of the money I threw in the stock market at the time. My wife and I knew, however, that if we lost that money, it wasn't going to affect our lives one bit. We could afford to take that risk. When you are answering my questions, if you are telling me that it's okay for me to take your money, invest it, and then lose it, then you are telling me that you are a gambler! And I have no desire to be your bookie!

People who are considered gamblers in the sense I just described are not interested in the 7 or 8 percent conservative gains per year that I give my clients. My numbers are not exciting to them; my numbers aren't something for gamblers to brag about at a cocktail party. They want to hear me say, "I'm really good. My minimum gain for a portfolio is 12 to 15 percent a year. I know inside stuff about the tech industry or any industry you can name." If I talked this way, I would be sprouting words from a big bag of hot air—just as I used to do and like most "investment professionals" out there who continue to peddle risk.

The truth is that no one in financial services has complete information to make constant gains of 12 to 15 percent. Even Bernie Madoff only promised 10 to 15 percent gains! The reason brokers can't live up to their pie-in-the-sky promises is that they are salesmen who do not know, understand, or control the information that develops behind their backs. They are at the bottom end of the Wall Street food chain and only play the role of information distributor to the firm's clients.

Furthermore, in the recent real estate bubble, lending institutions like Lending Tree, DiTech, WaMu, World Savings, and Countrywide were not going to tell their salesmen/brokers to slow down the volume of mortgages they churned out, even though the executives and salesmen on Wall Street knew that questionable loan underwriting was causing a dangerous, over-heated real estate market—the effects of which nearly threw the global economy into an unprecedented catastrophe.

For the reasons I've explained, I opted to leave a world of financial planning where inaccurate information sold intangible products that lost people money. The whole concept behind the Wall Street casino was foolish. There's a huge difference between knowledge, which I was peddling back at Kidder, Peabody (and which was incorrect more often than not), and wisdom. When it comes to investments, knowledge of this company's projections or that analyst's recommendations are overrated—because the information could be either bogus or only partially true. The thing to pursue is wisdom, which I define as discernment of what to do with people's money. The beginning of wisdom isn't greed for gains. It is understanding that the only people who make money in a casino … are the owners.

One of the primary investment vehicles of the last twenty-five years has been the 401(k). The problem is that as much as your employer (and your broker) wanted you to buy into the 401(k) concept, it just flat out didn't work. As an investment "vehicle," for all too many people, it's standing broken down by the side of the road, a smoking pile of junk. So how did you—and so many others—become convinced that the 401(k) was the way to go? Why did Wall Street and your employer team up to offer you this failed approach to retirement investing? And what can you do right now if you did have a 401(k) (or a 403(b) for government employees) that has lost much of its value? We'll turn to this critically important topic in the next chapter.

Chapter 3

Why Qualified Retirement Accounts Never Let You Retire

Remember Fred from Chapter 1? He has a 401(k) retirement account, put money into it every single month, and did exactly what the big boys on Wall Street told him to do. So why can't he ever retire comfortably?

Let's take a deeper look at 401(k) and other retirement plans that are funded with risk investments and find out why they make money for everybody involved with the plan … except the poor schnook who's putting his hard-earned money in. Amazingly, Fred thought he was contributing to his own retirement. Instead, for the last twenty years, he contributed to comfortable retirements for a whole lot of people in the financial services industry.

Fred worked his whole career for XYZ Corporation. When 401(k) plans came in, Fred enrolled because all the "smart people" whose books he read told him to do so. Some people he knew just kept their money in the bank. "How boring," Fred thought,

"They'll never have the money they need later on." Now it turns out that the boring people have more money than Fred. How could that have happened?

Every month for twenty years, through his 401(k) plan, Fred invested a portion of his income in stocks, bonds, or mutual funds, hoping that later on he could retire on the money he made on those investments. What Fred didn't know was that he was playing musical chairs with Wall Street. And he was losing the game from the day he started playing. The Wall Street executives, fund managers, and financial advisors were the players along with Fred. When the music stopped, they all got seats—because they knew when the music would stop. Poor Fred! Nobody ever took a moment to tell him when that moment would come.

From the mid-1980s to the present, Wall Street invited Fred and millions of other Americans to a game when billions of 401(k) dollars were put into the stock market ... and the real estate market. Wall Street executives should have known better. They should have known that mortgage-backed securities, which boosted the real estate market from 1999 to 2007, were potentially toxic in a real estate downturn (that is, the down cycles that have happened every ten to twelve years since 1945!). They likely saw the collapse of the real estate bubble coming. But they didn't say a thing to Fred about the risk that the mortgage-backed securities would have on the U.S. and international stock markets and Wall Street firms. Instead, his broker encouraged him to invest in stocks and mutual funds. Now, most of Fred's money is gone.

What's the cost? Fred's 401(k) plan now won't let him retire on time or with the same amount of resources to support the lifestyle he desired. Fred wasn't expecting to retire to the south of France and live in a castle overlooking the beach. He thought he'd be able to stay in his house, pay for his and his wife Janet's expenses after she quits teaching, play some golf, and maybe get a motor home to visit the grandchildren. But poor Fred can't afford to quit working now that his 401(k) has dropped by 40 percent.

What's the cause for Fred's financial mess? There are actually two basic reasons: 1) the replacement of his company's core retirement program with the 401(k) plan and 2) the greed of Wall Street that drove the economy into the real estate and tech bubbles and other financial meltdowns. Let's take a look and see how these things played out.

A History of Financial Flubs

From about 1940 to the mid-1980s, people working in the private sector secured their retirement through their company's core pension program. The core program was usually modeled similar to the government's defined benefits program, which stated that if you worked X amount of years, you would get Y amount of money as a pension in each year of your retirement. The defined benefits program was the deal that federal and state employees like teachers, policemen, and firemen received.

In the private sector, for employers like XYZ Corporation where Fred worked, it was the company's responsibility to fund and manage the core retirement programs and ensure that these were part of the corporation's assets. The federal government was only a retirement guarantor of last resort if the private company experienced bankruptcy, defaulted, or faced other major financial challenges or setbacks.

The government's bailout of Chrysler back in 1981 was an interesting example of this arrangement. Congress gave $1 billion in loan guarantees to Chrysler to revive its operations when the company was on its last legs. Congress opted to go that route rather than the more costly route of fulfilling its obligation to payout $1.5 billion for the company's pension plan in case of bankruptcy. But the Chrysler situation was very rare. Until then, most employers funded their pension plans appropriately and paid their retirees what they were owed.

As I mentioned in Chapter 2, my dad worked for Southern California Edison for 40 years and retired at age 60. Through his company's core retirement program, 60 percent of his salary was guaranteed at retirement for the rest of his life, adjusted to the increase in cost of living. In the early 1980s, he also enrolled in a savings supplemental 401(k) program that was supposed to assist him in making up the shortfall on the remaining 40 percent of his ending salary. In so doing, his lifestyle didn't have to change too much after retirement. While he worked, Dad would put aside a portion of his payroll to save up in that supplemental program, and he obtained a tax benefit for doing that. The 401(k) plan was the more prominent supplemental program enacted by Congress.

There was also the 403(b) plan for those people who worked for public education, churches, and non-profit organizations. Interestingly enough, from the introduction of 403(b) plans in 1963 to 1993 educators could only put annuities into their 403(B) plans. The Kennedy Administration mandated only safe, guaranteed investments for their plans. That changed in 1993 when

Congress opened up the 403(B) plans to mutual funds in addition to annuities with the same disastrous results for those who shifted from safety to risk.

These supplemental programs (IRAs, 401(k), 403(B), 457, etc.) were also called defined contribution programs: The Internal Revenue Service (IRS) defined how much you were able to put into those plans in addition to what was put into the core program of your company. The supplemental programs were great programs because they enabled workers like my dad to retire and still receive darn near the same amount of money they had received in salary.

Even if you didn't have money to put into the supplemental programs, you still had your core program, and you learned to live with what you got. Even when people lost money in the supplemental programs for whatever reason, they would still have a back-up core program. A back-up plan is always good!

So what happened? Why did my dad do so well ... and why did Fred do so poorly?

The key concept is that the corporate 401(k) plan and 403(b) plans for educators and government workers were never intended to be primary retirement plans! They were intended to be supplemental—to add to what your employer gave you in the core pension plan. Then things changed. In the early 1980s, Congress, the accounting industry, the Wall Street lobbyists, the mutual fund lobby, and the 401(k) plan administrator lobby got together and decided that it was too hard for corporations to fund core retirement programs. Their reasoning probably included the following points:

1. Why use the resources of the corporation to manage a retirement program when workers can do it themselves?
2. We need somebody to buy the common stocks of the companies for which we underwrite; why not have millions of corporate workers become the buyers?

They concluded that corporate workers should have a 401(k) plan where they would put a portion of their incomes in Wall Street investments that are supposed to grow to fund their retirement instead of a company's core retirement plan. So the 401(k) plan went from being a supplemental plan to becoming the primary retirement vehicle for millions of American workers. Corporations only had to partially match the worker's contributions—that is, if the worker could even afford to contribute. The companies then forced the employee to remain with the company 3, 5, or 10 years in order to be eligible to be vested to that employer match.

Through the urging of different highly compensated Wall Street and 401(k) lobbyists, private sector companies like Ford, Chrysler, and several of the largest domestic airlines decided to be rid of their core retirement programs and set up 401(k) plans for their workers. Over the next twenty-five years, more and more companies eliminated their core retirement programs while the state, county, and city governments retained them for their employees. Currently, fewer than 30 percent of American companies still have core retirement programs. The responsibility of funding retirement has slowly been shifting and placed on the backs of private sector workers—people like Fred.

Workers were sold on the 401(k) idea originally because we were told that we would have more control over our retirement money. The 401(k) salesmen told us, "Wouldn't it be better to control your own retirement account? You could put money in stocks, bonds, or mutual funds, and probably do better than whatever your company's core retirement plan offers. You can tailor your own plan to your own risk tolerance. Think of it! You can be in control of your own destiny! Of course, we'll charge a fee or two for all that … but still! You'll be the boss!"

How much control did workers really have? Did they have control over the fact that they lost money in stocks, bonds, and mutual funds in the 1987 stock market crash, during the recession of the early 1990s, during the tech bubble that burst around 2001, or during the recent economic meltdown? They had no control at any of those times!

In addition, how much control did workers really have over where they could invest their money through their 401(k) plans? They could only invest in stocks, bonds, and mutual funds that paid commissions and fees to financial services firms and funds. You couldn't stick your 401(k) money in any truly safe, risk-free investment like CDs or fixed insurance annuities. Why not? Because if you did, no one on Wall Street could make money off of you!

Would you like to put your 401(k) money in a bank CD? That's an investment guaranteed by the FDIC. Well, somehow, the 401(k) lobbyists and the rest of the Wall Street lobbyists excluded bank CDs from 401(k) plans. In fact, the lobbyists got Congress to say that we can't have products that have a back-end surrender charge (or a charge for pulling out funds before the completion of a certain period of time such as five years) on the menu for

Fred's investments. Wouldn't you know it? CDs have back-end surrender charges! Fixed annuities have back-end surrender fees! What a coincidence! The lobbyists probably used this justification: "We were just trying to protect Americans from getting charged on their investments in case they changed their minds or needed their money for unforeseen emergencies."

Well, so much for protection! While Wall Street was convincing Congress to set down these favorable restrictions for 401(k) plans (favorable to Wall Street!) in the early 1980s, CDs and fixed annuities earned 12 to 14 percent annually without risk, while the stock markets were hovering at Depression-era levels (adjusted for inflation). Wall Street desperately needed to figure out a way to bail itself out of a depressed market. It succeeded with the newfound supply of funds to purchase stocks and mutual funds through the 401(k) plans of the American worker.

When a downturn happens, the Freds of the world ask, "Why are there no Safe Money options in my retirement plan?" The harsh but simple answer is that Wall Street doesn't want Safe Money options like CDs and annuities because they won't make any money that way. If you can't use bank CDs and annuities for your 401(k) account, you are stuck with the tried and true casino games provided by Wall Street. With a fee here and a charge there, Wall Street firms stood to benefit enormously from 401(k) plans. And they did. They made millions and millions of dollars from charging your investment account, whether or not you made money.

So we see that the replacement of a company's core retirement plan was to Wall Street's financial benefit. They now receive money that was yours at one time; however, you bear all the risk—not your corporation (Wall Street's partner in crime is the company, who historically had to fund your retirement with conservative investments).

The Wall Street casino could take a devastating toll on 401(k) investments, even if the average Fred thinks that he played his cards right. Here is a rough summary of how the process works. A Wall Street firm goes to a company and says, "Hey, let us raise money for you by selling an interest in your company called a common stock." When a company agrees, the Wall Street firm has to sell the stock to somebody in order to raise funds for development and growth. Why not stick some stocks in mutual funds into Fred's 401(k) account as Fred monthly contributes to his plan under the direction of his plan's brokerage custodian? After all, Fred checked a box that indicated he had some tolerance for risk! Just how much risk is Fred bearing? Well, if Fred buys the stock or shares of the mutual fund, he owns 100 percent of the risk of the stock if it loses value. And he doesn't even know he bought the stock because his fund managers bought the stock for him. So the risk of the company's stock is borne not by the sharks on Wall Street but by the minnows on Main Street.

Mutual fund companies have a huge desire to purchase common stocks with the money in people's 401(k) accounts under their management. The fund advisors will call their investors like Fred and ask if they would like to invest in a utility fund that contains stocks from AT&T or Southern California Edison, tech funds, healthcare funds, or real estate funds. Wall Street is thrilled that mutual funds are doing billions of dollars of transactions in 401(k) accounts and taking not-too-informed orders from Fred.

Fred doesn't really know if he is investing in the right

companies. He is just listening to the advice of his advisors—who could be the low-paid clerks at the brokerage firm handling millions of inquiries nationwide or Fred's buddies in the lunchroom. Fred looks at his menu of investments and says, "Well, why don't I put some money in the Dow Jones, the S&P, this healthcare fund and that tech fund ..." Fred picks those investments with the same confidence he has trying to pick horses at the track; does he choose based on the bookie's information or "tout" sheets, the color of the jockey's shirt, or the lucky number of the horse?

Before 1982, less than 5 percent of the U.S. population owned stocks. Since 401(k) plans went from being supplemental to being the main retirement vehicle for millions of Americans, the biggest holders of stocks in this country are the Freds of the world who hold company stock and stock mutual funds in their 401(k) and other retirement accounts. Today, state pension funds such as the California Public Employees' Retirement System (CalPERS) have $215 billion invested, and 75 percent of the money is in stocks. (I was told by some actuaries of several state public employee pension funds, teachers' funds, and military funds that their funds need to make about 6 to 7 percent a year for a period of time in order to adequately fund everyone's retirement over time—40 percent drops are devastating to them and ultimately to taxpayers who must bail out those retirees!) Add to that the amount invested in the corporate stocks from other pension and mutual funds, and you witness an explosion in the stock market since the early '80s.

With the proliferation of 401(k) plans, stocks were sold at a higher volume, and they also had greater volatility—they could swing up or down more quickly with the emotional knee-jerk tendencies of the investing public. Before the explosion, the Dow

Jones Industrial Average was at 800 in 1982. These numbers turn out to be lower than the Dow in the 1930s when adjusted for inflation. However, as 401(k) plans gained popularity from 1983 on, we saw the Dow Jones go as high as 14,000 by October 2007 and then back down to 6,500 just eighteen months later (a loss of 53 percent) as we all painfully witnessed in early 2009. Even though the markets have gained 40 percent off their March 2009 lows, they are still, at this writing in October 2009, 35 percent below their peaks of just eighteen months ago.

Fred's participation, along with the participation of millions of other average folks, generated huge demand for common stocks. From 1984 to 1987, stocks grew in price. The Dow went from 800 in 1982 to over 2600 in 1987. Wall Street was elated because its firms made 2.5 percent and 3 percent annually in fees off your money invested in retirement plans ... whether you made money or not. And the mutual funds and brokerage firms make 25 to 30 percent of your account value over a ten-year period from your money peddling risk. Further subtract the bite of taxes on your gains, and you're lucky to be left with a 50 percent net of your imagined gains!

However, there's a reason why stocks are considered risky—there is always the chance that you will lose big. All of a sudden, in October 1987, the Dow dropped 33 percent in two weeks from 2600 to 1739. That was, to say the least, devastating!

Before that crisis, a lot of people who bought stocks borrowed against the rising value of their stocks to buy new houses or cars, take vacations, and invest in businesses. They might have borrowed up to 70 or 80 percent of the value of stock portfolio. These people woke up one day and discovered their stocks were down about 30 percent. Then came many margin calls: Brokers demanded that these investors put more money in their portfolios or sell some assets to make up the loss. Many people got wiped out in late 1987 because of the added pressure of folks having to sell their stocks when they didn't have more cash to put into their accounts.

After that experience, people wanted to be more careful, so it took several years before the market returned to a bullish attitude. Then around the mid-90s, we saw a buying frenzy stoked by a Wall Street-created bubble in the tech industry. The bubble involved thousands companies that had no sales, no revenues, and no earnings per share. Wall Street analysts made up stories about the viability of these companies. All of a sudden, you called your brokerage firm, whether it was Fidelity or Schwab or another large firm, and you asked, "What's up? What's hot?" And they would tell you about the tech stocks. You might then rush to get out of the secure blue-chip stocks and jump into the tech stocks, investing $100,000 or even over a million dollars because you didn't want to miss the boat! As always, it's your fear of missing the gains or getting the losses versus Wall Street's greed for making money whether you do or not—and all of it fueled by worry created by Wall Street's engine of misinformation.

From 2000 to 2003, the market went down almost 46 percent because it was obsessed with tech stocks that had absolutely no value. Probably 80 percent of tech companies involved in the bubble went out of business, and investors lost the majority of their investments. The 401(k) account holders got cleaned out of a boatload of money from 2000 to 2003. How could I even put people's anger into words? That would take another book!

From 2003 to 2007, the market finally got back to where it was in early 2000: It gained 60 percent off its 2002 lows. But we had a new bubble; this time it was called real estate. Once again Wall Street fueled the engine of greed. Real estate grew so dramatically during that time that Wall Street got together with the banks and created instruments called "Collateralized Debt Obligations" (CDO's). Wall Street said to the banks, "Hey, we've got a great deal for you. Put together as many loans as you can—hundreds of thousands of them. We'll break them up, package them, and sell them to pension funds, mutual funds, foreign governments and the general public in their 401(k) plans. You make huge fees and bonuses—we make huge fees and bonuses—and guess who assumes all the risk for this new casino game?"

This CDO party went on for years, and things got so overheated that lending institutions loaned money to people who could not have qualified for a loan under normal, prudent underwriting standards. But now, many of these people qualified for a loan for home purchases by just having a pulse! Nearly everyone qualified for a home loan from 2000 to 2007 as the lax underwriting of the greedy lenders didn't even check to see if they had jobs!

For example, at the insistence of Congress during 2002-2007 to help low-income families to partake in the explosion in real estate prices, loans were made available to people in low-income communities in Southern California and other parts of the country who could not afford to repay those loans. It seems that nobody at any of the lending institutions involved in peddling the mortgage-backed CDOs did the basic prudent mortgage underwriting or reality checks to ensure that the people to whom they lent were able to qualify and repay the loans. Easy money always creates an over-bought environment—whether in stocks or real estate!

Wall Street likes to keep pushing stocks until the end of the line even after the firms made their fees, executives exercised their stock options, and the analysts received their bonuses. The real estate bubble fueled easy money, easy credit, and improper underwriting. Now banks like Countrywide, WaMu (now Chase), IndyMac and Wachovia are bailed out for Wall Street's and the lender's greed after 401(k) holders lost 40 to 50 percent of their money in the stock market, while seeing their real estate values plunge 30-40 percent in just two short years. So the executives of the lending institutions and Wall Street got theirs—but what about Fred? You guessed it ... he's left holding the bag, a bag which contains about 40 percent less money than it did a year ago!

Some firms were also pushed to the edge of sanity. Follow me closely on this one. The giant insurer AIG thought it was taking advantage of an opportunity and getting a piece of the CDO pie when it proposed to reinsure the market value of mortgage securities to the institutional investors who bought them. Wall Street responded, "Great! Now we have an exit strategy for an overheated market." Suddenly, when the real estate bubble burst and investors of CDOs lost money, AIG had to honor insurance contracts for the purchasers of the mortgage securities. But AIG couldn't honor all the contracts because even though it had assets, it didn't have time to sell off other assets to obtain the cash to pay its reinsurance obligations on those toxic mortgage pools. AIG formed a new game in the Wall Street casino, and it lost.

Before the bubble, the AIG life insurance and annuity divisions were (and continue to be) as solid as they can be. AIG made hundreds of millions of dollars in fees on insurance and annuity premiums. So it didn't need to play the CDO game, but it did so because of greed. The U.S. government had little choice but to bail out AIG because the company was so big that its failure might have taken down the entire global economy. But where's Fred's bailout? Nowhere, of course!

After the real estate bubble had burst in mid-2007, there was a lot of finger pointing. The truth is the real estate bubble represented a new game of chance that formed in the Wall Street casino. Organizations such as AIG and WaMu participated in the game of chance, and everyone lost this time—not just Fred. But only Fred took a lasting hit. Because the Federal Reserve was never going to bail out Fred! Instead, what was left of Fred's hard-earned cash (turned into tax dollars) was used to bail out the very institutions that had nearly destroyed the economy in the first place!

When 401(k) and Wall Street lobbyists convinced Congress and the Department of Labor during the 1980s that CDs and life insurance annuities (which guarantee principal during accumulation and a lifetime income) weren't a good idea for Fred's menu of investment options for his 401(k) plan, they were not looking out for Fred's interest. Now Fred calls his advisor, who is one of those good-old boys on Wall Street, and says, "I'm 65 years old. I can't afford to lose any more money. What options have you got for me?"

The only option that the advisor has for Fred is to put his money in bond funds, which are considered less risky than stock funds. But just how safe are bond funds? During the stock market debacle of 2008 and 2009, the average bond fund went down 15 percent. It is absolutely criminal that Fred has no Safe Money options! Compared with stock funds, it was slightly less of a beating. But was it justifiable? No way!

Let's take another look back in history. As we discussed earlier, the stock market was so bad during the 1930s recession that it took about 25 years, until 1954, for the Dow-Jones Industrial Average to get back to where it was in 1929. In fact, if you had put your money in a bank or other conservative investment that only gave you 4.7 percent per year, you would have matched the performance of the Dow from 1929 to 1973! Now, you might ask yourself, what's the point of trying to pick the best funds and the best stocks in the first place if all I needed along the way is just a 4.7 percent annual return on my investments? Good question! It sure isn't worth the lost sleep and ulcers!

From 1996 to 2003, only 24 percent of mutual fund managers outperformed the leading indexes—Nasdaq, S&P 500, and Dow Jones. Doesn't it make more sense to just put money in the indexes through no-load mutual funds and let them do what they do instead of spending all that time, money, and resources trying to find the next hot fund or market sector? Study after independent study proves that you will beat the professionals 76 percent of the time! Wouldn't your bookie like those odds?

After the last six years, 90 percent of professionals did not beat the indexes. In addition, even in desperate times, financial advisors were still not giving advice in their clients' best interest. In 2007 and 2008, financial advisors actually encouraged people to go into the Chinese and Indian stock markets when things started slowing down in the American market. But once people set foot into Asian waters, they drowned, and their stocks went down 60 percent while our market went down 50 percent. It's almost like the financial advisors ensured that you didn't miss the opportunity to lose more money in the Chinese casino!

In a segment that aired in the spring of 2009, Steve Kroft from CBS's 60 Minutes interviewed the leading 401(k) plan lobbyist to Congress and asked how they could allow these losses to happen. He smugly answered that the problem wasn't created by the 401(k) administration industry; the problem lies with the investment community! In other words, Wall Street!

The lobbyist also stated that people like Fred should have known that they were putting money at risk when they put money in their 401(k) mutual funds. With that answer, Steve Kroft's mouth dropped open. Where was the conscience in that answer? How do the financial wizards of Wall Street sleep at night, disavowing any responsibility for having destroyed the retirement dreams of the millions of investors who trusted them?

The bottom line is that even though the stock market has begun to rise again after this devastating loss of wealth, don't get too excited. You are still charged fees. Your money is still at risk. Chances are that the market will never go up enough to recoup the losses you suffered in the past—especially if you don't have a lock-in mechanism to handle the possibility of future downturns. In addition, Wall Street will most certainly come up with another market-frenzied bubble, maybe this time in commodities like oil or metals that certainly should go up because of the devaluation of our currency after the extreme increase of the money supply by the Fed to prevent a global meltdown. Wall Street will regenerate the public's appetite for risk and entice Congress to stay the course with the present 401(k) plan structure instead of allowing the public to shift their 401(k) menu options to safe savings programs prior to age fifty-nine and a half.

We can only conclude that Wall Street and their 401(k) system is just one vicious shark frenzy tank. Millions of Freds are dropped into the tank but don't know why they are in the tank or how they got there. That's why you will never be able to retire with peace of mind from possible future catastrophic losses…as long as the current flawed investment system remains in place.

So if the 401(k) plan doesn't work, what will? What do you really need in order to create a retirement that Wall Street can't destroy? You need three things: knowledge, understanding, and control over your own retirement savings. You need to have the flexibility of being able to invest in Safe Money options not offered by your employer's 401(k) plan.

I'll now describe for you the Safe Money alternatives, so you can learn how to protect your money. And, Fred, if you're reading, I have good news. It's not too late to save your retirement dreams … if you take the advice you'll find in the next chapter.

Chapter 4

Safe Money and the Power of Indexing

We now know that the 401(k) isn't a surefire ticket to retirement security unless the investments in it are safe. But what is safe? I suggest the Safe Money System™. It has worked for my clients, and I'm certain it will work for you.

Let me start with how I converted to the Safe Money philosophy. As I told you, I left Wall Street in 1983 at the dawning of the era of the 401(k). I started working with public educators. Unlike my previous clients with mutual funds in their 401(k)s, teachers had 403(b) plans, which by law could not include mutual funds. As a result, the 401(k) took on all the risk of the mutual funds while the 403(b) seemed risk free.

In the early '80s, since my clients couldn't get into mutual funds, they invested in CDs and fixed annuities. I thought it was especially interesting that certain CDs and fixed annuities had annual returns of 12 to 15 percent and that the principal on these financial products was guaranteed. My clients' investments were safely growing and guaranteed to be there, no matter the conditions on Wall Street. On the other hand, the stock market was at historical lows, and investors who had bet their money on risky securities and mutual funds were losing money left and right.

After seeing the growth of my client's money with no thanks to Wall Street, I thought to myself, why bother with risk? Why bother with the risky funds on Wall Street when I made money for my clients and didn't lose money? I consistently gave my clients 7 to 9 percent annual returns over the last two decades.

After seeing the downturn in the '80s and the burst of the Wall Street-created tech bubble in the late '90s, I thought, "Why put my clients through the rollercoaster ride on Wall Street, when I can smooth sail them into retirement—risk free and drama free?"

I was led to the Safe Money philosophy through the revelation that making money without incurring risk is possible. In fact, it is just silly to play with risk when you don't have to or may be harmed by doing so.

When I started my own independent retirement consultancy, My Retirement Coach, I was fortunate not to have to deal with Wall Street. No more trying to pick the next hot stock or the next big fund! Moreover, I was not involved with the 401(k) plan system except when I worked with clients who could transfer their 401(k) funds to IRA funds. My clients and I were spared the danger of the Wall Street casino.

In 1993, legislation changed and allowed mutual funds to extend their services to those with the 403(b) plan, which created more demand for stocks. Of course, when that happened, some of my clients found the returns of the stock market tempting since people who were already in the market were temporarily making 20 to 30 percent annual returns on their investments from 1997 to 1999. However, I managed to steer my clients away from the hypnotizing bright lights of the Wall Street casino. I refused to get sucked back in and stayed with Safe Money. It was the right decision: The stock markets decreased 46 percent during 2000 through 2002; everyone gave up all those gains and then some.

The Idea Behind Indexing

So what's the Safe Money System all about? What are the specifics of my approach to investing?

A lot of people hope that in the future, someone may be smart enough to create a financial product with the potential to only give investors gains and never losses. What Wall Street doesn't tell you, or is afraid to tell you, is that such a product already exists. My clients have been using it since 1998; it's called the "Fixed Index Annuity."

The fixed index annuity is basically a contract with an insurance company. The insurance company says to you, "Give us some money, and we'll guarantee that your principal investment will never be lost. And you will receive either a stated annual interest rate or participate with us in the growth of the stock market without risk of loss." They have been making and keeping that promise of principal protection to their clients for over 120 years!

Pretend that you gave the insurance guys $100 to invest this year in a fixed index annuity. They guarantee that you will not lose the $100, and you choose whether you want to receive the declared interest rate for one year (say, 4 percent) or to participate in the gains of a stock market index (like the Dow, S&P 500, or Nasdaq). The insurance guys, just like the bank guys, are in the business of making money on your money at no risk to them. If the stock index goes up 10 percent for the year, you would get about 70 percent of the gains, and they would pocket the difference. So your $100 investment would now have grown to $107.

If the market is down, you don't make anything (nor do they), but you don't lose anything either. You then take your same account value and go on to the next year. The insurance companies accomplish this security by buying one-year options on that index. If the markets gain, everyone wins. If they markets lose, the insurance company only loses on the cost of the option. In either case, you don't lose any value for your account. This strategy is called indexing, and you will never lose money using it!

The beauty of indexing using the fixed index annuity is that your gains will be "locked-in" each year and shielded from the shocks and falls in the stock market. As I mentioned, your principal of $100 and the $7 you will make on it the next year comes to a total of $107. This $107 balance will be locked-in going forward, and you will not lose it, even though you might not make any more money the year after due to a downturn in the markets. Your principal and the earnings on your principal are guaranteed! I'm sure you can see the huge contrast between this lock-in feature in the fixed index annuity and the lack of this feature in mutual funds!

In 1963, when the Kennedy administration formulated the 403(b) plans for educators, the only investment option allowed for the 403(b) was a fixed annuity. Aside from U.S. Treasuries, fixed annuities were considered the safest option in which to invest. I have clients who started their retirement accounts back in the '60s, and to this day, they haven't lost any money because of the fixed annuity products in their 403(b) plans. Even in the terrible market downturn of the 1980s, they made 12 to 15 percent a year and slept very well at night!

It's extremely important to remember that we're talking about fixed annuities, not variable annuities. I don't like a variable annuity (where stock mutual funds are wrapped in an insurance contract blanket) as an investment strategy for one's "can't afford to lose' retirement funds. I'm OK with market risk for discretionary funds where one's lifestyle won't be diminished if they lose principal. But I just don't find many people who can afford to lose money, let alone the money to fund their retirement dreams.

In other words, my advice is to choose products that offer the safety and guarantees of traditional fixed annuities. For this reason, the fixed index annuity was born out of the desire of the insurance companies to compete against Wall Street for management of retirement funds. The competing edge for insurance companies is that they can secure your principal and the earnings on your principal from loss, while Wall Street cannot do so in the stock market.

Over the last 15 years, the insurance industry provided our clients better performance than the stock brokerage firms because of the unique annual lock-in feature of the fixed annuities. My clients did not experience the stock market taking back their gains during the devastating market collapses of 2000-2003, and 2008-2009. As I mentioned in Chapter 1, market losses hurt you far greater than gains help you; a 50% loss needs a 100% gain to get back to even!

I hope you believe what I have to say about the benefits of fixed annuities, but it's always nice to have some real world backup. How about the Wharton School of Business? It's one of the most respected business schools in the world; the Wharton Financial Institutions Center completed a study in October 2009 entitled "Real World Index Annuity Returns." They wanted to determine just how beneficial annuities were for real people because most of the studies that had already been published were either pro-annuity (if they were paid for by the annuities industry) or anti-annuity (if they had been produced for the securities industry). No surprise there! Here's what the authors of the independent study determined:

The reality is at least some index annuities have produced returns that have been truly competitive with Certificates of Deposit, fixed rate annuities, taxable bond funds, and even equities at times. ... How will index annuities perform in the future? We do not know but the concept has proven to work in the past and any articles should reflect this. ... The FIA is designed for safety of principal with returns linked to upside market performance.

If I say it, you may or may not believe it. But now you've got Wharton saying the same thing, and I think you can count on their objective analysis.

Similar to the insurance companies' fixed annuity business, commercial banks also ensure that your deposits and the earnings on your deposits will not be lost. That explains why commercial banks and insurance companies are typically among the largest, strongest, and securest financial institutions in the world. Now, I'm not talking about banks and insurance companies that jumped on the risk wagon and traveled past the speed limit, such as those involved with creating and packaging toxic mortgage-backed securities. Those greedy knuckleheads thought they could create excessive fees by loosening their underwriting standards for real estate loans and then make additional fees by packaging and selling the toxic, over-valued mortgage pools to another set of knuckleheads called Wall Street. Now 80 percent of them are out of business—or would be, if our tax dollars hadn't bailed out their sorry backsides!

Take one more look at the difference between Wall Street firms and insurance companies. Wall Street makes money whether you do or not, and when the ship's going down, the captain is the first in the lifeboat called bailout money, while you never get to the lifeboat! Who bailed you out? Commercial banks and insurance companies typically make money with you—not in spite of you.

Suddenly, blue-chip firms like Merrill Lynch, Fidelity, and TD Ameritrade are touting retirement plans similar to the fixed annuity products offered by insurance companies for around a hundred years. They do so because they have to regain their reputation of being able to manage and grow retirement funds and not lose funds as they did in the recent decade-long downturn. What I have to say to them is this: How the heck are you going to regain your reputation after you have already lost half of people's money? You only want them to stay at risk in your casino in order to try to recover their losses. Likewise, casino blackjack dealers love it when you think you have to double down your bets in order to hit the big pot to make up for your earlier losses.

The Safe Money System involves accumulating money in a safe way, never losing what you accumulated, and coming up with a plan that will pay you out for as long as you live because you don't want to outlive your money. In addition, it's learning to live the "Enough" lifestyle. For our clients, the fixed index annuity is doing a great job keeping their money safe with its lock-in mechanism for their annual returns and guaranteed annual payments during retirement. Their assets don't fluctuate wildly based on Wall Street's whims, and they are worry free from the devastating stress and emotional damage that overtakes people who don't escape the gambling mentality. Our clients have control of their money, and the peace of mind to pursue the relationships and activities that they dreamed of during their working years.

Wall Street's Dirty Little Secret

If a fixed annuity is so great, then why aren't more people putting their money into it? The reason is the marketing and sales agenda of its opponents. Wall Street has always told you that you don't want annuities because insurance companies are charging large surrender fees. Surrender fees apply when you change your mind and want to take your money out of the annuity before the completion of the five to ten-year period dictated by your contract. If there is an unforeseen emergency that requires you to take money out of your fixed annuity, things become inconvenient because you lose a percentage of your money. Now you know that's the catch of a fixed annuity. But that's a lot better than living with all the risk!

There are also scenarios where a fixed annuity is just outright dangerous. Imagine Charles, a seventy-five-year-old man in small town mid-America (where houses cost $80,000 to $250,000). He has only $50,000 to his name and nothing but Social Security to support him. (By the way, Social Security was created with the same mentality as 401(k) accounts—it was meant to be supplemental, not the primary source of retirement income.)

Now Charles wants someone to help him manage his $50,000. An advisor comes along and sells him a fixed annuity contract. Months later, Charles wants to take his money out of the annuity but only gets $45,000 back because of surrender fees. That is a criminal situation where the advisor was a salesman who didn't care for the well-being of his client. Still, at least the poor guy didn't lose all of his money when the stock market crashed in 1999—because he was in a fixed annuity. We see that even when an inappropriate fixed annuity recommendation occurs, it is still—in the bigger picture—better than a recommendation for a risky mutual fund.

I hope I'm clear that there are downsides to fixed annuities—no investment is perfect. I do want you to see that the surrender charge is just one negative compared to many positives. People buy a fixed annuity because they want three good things to happen: a lifetime income solution to pay for life's needs, guaranteed principal to insure that the income from the annual payouts doesn't run out too soon, and flexibility to take out the invested money if needed during your working years. To alleviate the inconvenience of surrender fees, I stress distributing your investments into CDs and treasuries, in addition to fixed annuities, so that you have other liquid sources of money.

If at some point down the road you need to pay surrender fees, you might be relieved to hear that the fees might just come from the growth value of the annuity. Of course, there is the chance that the fees dig into the principal; for example, you might be forced to pay 10 percent on a principal of $100,000 when your investment has only grown to $105,000. However, think about the people with 401(k)s, who didn't put their money in fixed annuities and are losing many times the value of your surrender fees due to losses in stock value. Moreover, there's only a 7 to 8 percent upfront and one-time commission that you pay the insurance companies to start a fixed annuity contract (although your account is credited with 100 percent of your deposit, unlike stock mutual funds). Compare that with the 2.5 to 3 percent commission fee that you pay Wall Street year after year after year.

Ten years in a mutual fund or managed stock account means between 25 and 30 percent came off your account value whether you made money or not! I'm sure you'll agree with me that the potential risk of loss at the Wall Street casinos and the accompanying stress overshadows any commissions charged on a fixed annuity. Solid advice that causes your accounts to gain without stress and grief over many years should be worth the commission that the insurance company (not you) pays me.

Another thing keeping people from getting into fixed annuities is the warning of some well-known financial advisors to never put an annuity in a tax-deferred qualified retirement account because the annuity growth is already tax deferred. A qualified retirement plan is a plan that meets certain requirements of the Internal Revenue Code and thus receives certain tax benefits like tax deferral. This means that the growth on your annuity will not be taxed until you withdraw the money. (In contrast, you pay taxes on the growth of your CDs even though you never withdrew the money you put in the CDs.) Some advisors would say that there is no use in putting a tax-deferred product in a tax-deferred account. Well, I say who cares what the tax status is as long as you are making money! Do you really care about the tax debate if the only other option is to lose big money with other, riskier options? Everything that comes out of a qualified retirement account is taxed anyway—just ensure that there's something left in there to be withdrawn!

The Truth about Bonds

You might be saying, "Okay, Randy. I get your point about fixed annuities. But what about bonds? Aren't bonds safe?" Great question!

I like to say that Wall Street is an "accumulation entity." In other words, Wall Street is in the business of accumulating assets. What Wall Street never figured out is this: Now that the money is there, what can be done to pay it out efficiently? In other words, they've never developed a lifetime income solution without any loss of principal for those who put their hard-earned dollars into risky investments. Wall Street's solution is usually bond funds because they typically pay periodic interest payments to its investors and are considered safer than stocks—that is, until the recent meltdown of the worldwide financial system threatened to bankrupt even the strongest corporations whose bonds are held in the trillions by mutual funds and pensions.

The problem with bond funds is that when interest rates rise, the value of your principal goes down. In that case, your principal is stuck in the bond fund and is prevented from growing in the high-interest-rate-induced market. As a result, there will be selling pressure on you to dump bonds and go into stocks or bond funds with greater risk and higher returns. But now your likelihood of losing money becomes greater. The majority of bond funds lost 12 to 15 percent in 2008 alone.

A few brave souls might venture to ask their financial advisors if there are investment options that have a sort of lock-in mechanism that would prevent losses. The advisor might think of fixed annuities, U.S. Treasury bond funds, or bank CDs but will never say a thing about them because the firm's executive team and analysts only care about touting stocks. The performance—and paycheck—of the typical investment advisor is based on the amount of stocks he sells or funds he places under management, not on how much safety and peace of mind he creates for his clients. The advisor would tell you to get into this stock or fund because the analysts tell the sales force and the public to do so.

Does this scenario sound familiar? It will strike a chord with many people who listened to such advice and lost tens of thousands. These losses should signal that it is time to leave the Wall Street casino.

Leaving their Wall Street brokerage houses to follow the Safe Money System and invest in a fixed annuity is not easy for many investors. Some people have developed tight relationships with their stockbrokers because these brokers have taken them out to lunch or dinner and sent them champagne at Christmas. As a result, they might feel obligated to stay with their brokers, not willing to make anyone feel bad or feel guilty for losing your money. But the truth is, all of us in the retirement planning business are salesmen, and it's our job to be personable people or else we won't succeed. Don't be fooled by sales pitches and proposals of friendship, and don't hesitate to say that you don't want your advisor's advice anymore. For God's sake, let them stay your friend, but quit enabling your "friend" to gamble with your life's savings.

I can tell you this—if my family doctor operated on my kids several times, and there were continual catastrophic results, I'd be sure to get a new doctor! Wouldn't you? Well, your financial advisor is your "money doctor," and their job is to make you healthy—not sick to your stomach!

Moreover, many investors fail to set boundaries about what they can or cannot afford to lose. These people are afraid to admit that they are not in control of their money because their brokers rule over it with an iron fist. Fearful of facing reality, some are not even looking at their statements and realizing that they are not getting the 10 percent annual returns on their investments as their broker had told them. After all the management fees, commissions, and taxes, what was said to be 10 percent might actually be 6 percent per year. And remember you pay the freight even if you lose money!

The bottom line is that you need to examine closely the numbers that your advisor throws at you and make the decision that's best for you not for your advisor about whether to stay with or leave your current brokerage house.

Does the Safe Money System Really Work?

Let's look at the following case study to understand how to apply the Safe Money System if you have a 401(k) plan. You probably don't know when you can retire. And you don't know what your Safe Money options are while you are still working. Here's an interesting fact for you. In 2006, Congress enacted legislation that allowed people who are still working for their companies and still contributing to their 401(k) plans to transfer the bulk of their principal in their company's 401(k) to self-directed IRAs, where they are able to invest in products like a fixed annuity or another guaranteed savings vehicle. Employees can only do this if they are over fifty-nine and a half years old. The purpose of this legislation is to give people more control, flexibility, and choice concerning their investments but still allow them to continue to work with their employer. They can continue to contribute to their existing 401(k) even if they transfer money out of it to a self-directed IRA to lock-in and protect their investment portfolio.

This setup is called an in-service distribution because when you transfer your funds out, you can still be working for the company. Currently, about 70 percent of American corporations provide for an in-service distribution. Ask your company's 401(k) plan administrator if you are eligible to take advantage of this great tool to protect your retirement dreams.

Another important thing to know if you are under fifty-nine and a half years old is that if you have left your company and go to work for another, you can still move funds in the 401(k) plan of your old company to an IRA plan. If you left your 401(k) with the old company's 401(k) administrator, you are eligible to transfer it to an IRA, regardless of your age. Many people are not aware of this fact. That action is not an in-service distribution; it is considered a 401(k) rollover triggered by termination of employment. There are potentially millions of such rollovers eligible for transfer in the late 2000s, considering the countless job losses and job transfers.

Remember, an in-service distribution allows only those who are fifty-nine and a half years and over to participate. If you are "underage" (I bet nobody's called you that for a while!), then we would need to address the best options for you to get money out of exposure to risky markets within your current plan's menu options. You may wish to go into a bond fund where there may be less return but less risk by telling the 401(k) custodian to reduce your exposure to risk.

My retirement consultancy has always been able to give an accurate assessment of where somebody is going to be financially in ten, fifteen, or twenty years. Can Wall Street do that? Are you kidding me?! I think you know the answer to that one by now! So how are we able to do that? Well, the financial products that we use have historically given us a predictable 7 percent-annual return over the past twenty years. You probably realize that your money doubles every ten years at 7 percent. What has your portfolio done over the last ten years?

Let's say you're fifty years old, and you plan to retire at sixty-five. You have wisely come to me to ask me to manage your money with the Safe Money System. I can take out a simple handheld calculator and predict with pretty good accuracy what you will have in your retirement account fifteen years from now. I can not only calculate what you will accumulate based on 7 to 8 percent annual returns (based on verifiable historical performance for your investments) but also project what your Social Security, real estate portfolio, and other pension plans will generate in income for you—and for how long.

You then give me $500,000 to put into a retirement account. Let me be modest and say that if I could get you a steady 5 percent annual return on that money, I would be able to double your money to $1,000,000 in just fourteen years. At retirement, you could even take out 7 percent or $70,000 each year, and this income stream will last you about twenty-five years. I can make all these calculations for you with no problem—with a $50 handheld HP calculator! Financial wisdom is not predicated on sophisticated, complicated technology. Numbers are your best friend, as long as the numbers aren't going down…and as long as they make sense to you!

This process that I just went through with you is so simple that it doesn't make sense to go to Wall Street for your retirement needs. Why stress yourself out in the Wall Street casino with its complicated risk games and unpredictability when my Safe Money System can lay your financial future out in front of you clear and simple?

To put it even more simply, the Safe Money System follows the Golden Rule, which I will put this way: Do for others what you wish to have done for you. In this case, the rule means that when someone recommends a financial product to a client, he or she should think, "Would I recommend this product or strategy to my best friend or my mother?" If you are the client, don't be shy to ask the guy at the other side of the desk, "Would you put your mom in this?" Ask them if their life savings and retirement future are in this investment or strategy.

And my answer to that question? Yes. My wife and I have the majority of our life savings in these strategies as do my mom, stepmom, and best friend. Every single client of mine has their financial well-being tied to these strategies!

I've been in the retirement business long enough to promise you that the majority of Wall Street bookies do not own a large position in the stocks and funds that they recommend to you based on their firm's research. The reason is that they know the game, and they know the risk. They also know that Wall Street hits a down cycle every five to seven years, causing any stock that they recommend now to plummet—regardless of the fundamental touted by the research analysts—because when the public panics, everything goes down! And every bookie with over twenty years experience knows what it feels like to see the disappearance of his/her client base due to the confiscation of money by Wall Street's greed and shenanigans. More than likely, these stockbrokers themselves can't even afford to buy the same stocks that they recommend to others because they too have lost money in stocks or they've had their earning reduced drastically when the casinos came crashing down. And they are advising you?

If you want the same retirement investment system that the person recommending it to you is using, then you should go with Safe Money. And if you like casinos, stay away from Wall Street and go to Las Vegas. At least there, when you're losing your money, you can still catch a buffet and a show!

In this chapter, I want to share with you the foundation of the Safe Money System. It rests on four principals or pillars, so you can clearly see the strength of the system and why it can last forever.

Chapter 5

The Four Pillars of a Worry-Free Financial Plan

Taking the worry out of financial planning is one of my greatest gifts to my clients. I'm not performing magic. I'm just following the four-pillar investment approach of the Safe Money System, and I'd like to describe them for you now. The four pillars of Safe Money are as follows:

1. Guarantee the safety of your principal;
2. Control and flexibility of your money;
3. A crediting method for growth on your money based on participation in the stock market gains, but not the losses; and
4. A lock-in mechanism that secures the growth of your account value to prevent losses during a future downturn.

Let's see how each of these will have a highly positive effect on your financial life.

The First Pillar: Guarantee

In today's world, most people think of the idea of guaranteed principal as wishful thinking. What do you mean "guaranteed principal?" Get out of town! It's impossible! The idea is almost bizarre to people who have lost large amounts of their principal in the stock market. So it takes a while for me to convince some of these individuals that it is possible to have a lucrative investment in which the principal is completely protected and completely guaranteed.

People were led to believe by Wall Street that in order to have a proper or aggressive return on their investment, they must be involved in some risk. In fact, society now correlates risk directly with return: More risk equals more return. If someone doesn't want to bear risk, he is considered the social outcast—the bench-sitter. He's ostracized socially. All his friends at the club brag about the risky nature of their investments because somehow that translates in their minds into being bold, swaggering, and success oriented. Can you hear Wall Street asking you, "What's the matter, not tough enough?"

Of course, it never occurs to people that the "risk" part of the risk/reward equation might actually happen to them and that they will lose some or most of their hard-earned money. But they sure have in the last couple of years. Now they aren't bragging about risk anymore!

So, now that risk is a little less desirable, what types of investments exist that guarantee the safety of the principal? Investors who choose to avoid risk have limited options on Wall Street. They can either invest in CDs or bonds—products which don't yield much return. Consequently, less return means less money to retire on. If that happens to you, then you should be afraid, very afraid. By investing in CDs or bonds, you're really guaranteeing yourself losses—because the meager rate of return on those investments will never keep pace with inflation. That's especially true in light of the greater inflation rates we can all expect in years to come.

Wall Street knows that deep down many investors are gamblers and actually crave risk. They prey on our fears that we won't have enough and that safe investments are all doomed to failure. (At least, the safe investments they offer are doomed!) So their ads, which appear to focus on offering you a great retirement through their investment products, are really intended to induce fear. If Wall Street succeeds in inducing fear in you, then they succeeded in their marketing and sales campaign to get you to invest in risky securities with them.

The big investment companies want clients to fear that they aren't making enough money so they have to invest with more risk, or that they will lose money if they don't invest and thus miss a golden opportunity. I don't call watching the Dow sliced in half in a matter of months a golden opportunity for investors, but they don't worry about your returns as long as you place your money under their control. Instead, they want you to fret that the train is leaving the station; you are either on it too late or too soon. If you are on it too soon, you should have waited for more risk to come along before getting on board with your investments. If you are on it too late, you watch everyone else make money while you are left behind. Either way, Wall Street wins by getting your money. The bottom line is that Wall Street has to continually inject worry into the mindset of the public.

Every time you jump into the risk wagon with Wall Street, it's going to dump a lot of "wastepaper securities" on you. I define wastepaper securities as "the investments that knowledgeable investors are too smart to fall for." With this trend of "you jumpin' and them dumpin'," it is not a surprise that the principal you put into your investments is almost guaranteed … to deteriorate if not evaporate altogether. When deterioration happens, people begin to lose hope of ever finding financial products that would guarantee a safe principal.

Now is the time that we pick ourselves up from the ashes and look for financial products that satisfy our first Safe Money requirement of guaranteed principal. We covered the first steps in the previous chapters: doing your history homework to see what kinds of returns are realistic; finding the financial products that could get you those returns; and most importantly, protecting your principal investment. In addition, we have to understand what kinds of cycles and bubbles exist on Wall Street that would backfire on the investments we make and what kinds of products could be immune from the same dangers.

Guaranteed principal is a must-have necessity to ensure that you have enough money with which to retire. You contribute to your retirement funds year after year and delay gratification so that you can enjoy life later. You shouldn't let Wall Street make your efforts worthless.

As we've seen, the one investment that definitely guarantees your principal is a fixed index annuity. My clients have never experienced a loss of their principals with this approach. Their principals are guaranteed by the financial strength of some of the largest, most stable insurance companies in the world, such as Allianz Life, Old Mutual, ING, Aviva, and North American Life. Over the last 120 years, no policyholder of a life or annuity contract has lost one dime of their original principal on their savings plans with these companies. They are rated by AM Best, Standard and Poors, and Moody based on the quality of their investment portfolio (which is primarily in investment grade bonds and government securities and mortgages) and by how much surplus over potential claims they have. All of the companies mentioned above (and most other A-rated or better companies) have between 130-160 percent surplus cash to potential claims for cash redemptions on their life and annuity policies. How much surplus do you think your bank has? Zero, and that's why they need the FDIC to cover any liquidity problems when there's a run on the bank!

The guarantees for my clients are not only on the original savings principal but also on the future account values that have grown from interest crediting. During the negative years in the stock market, my clients make nothing, but during the positive years, they make about 60-70 percent of the gains made on Wall Street. Their gains are also locked-in along with their principal to prevent losses down the road as they approach retirement so that their lifetime incomes will not be diminished. We will discuss the importance of this lock-in mechanism later on.

The Second Pillar: Control and Flexibility

Now let's turn to the second core aspect of the Safe Money System: the issue of control and flexibility. Having control and flexibility over your retirement planning isn't just about having a 401(k) plan but also about controlling your real estate portfolio and your other savings programs. In addition, you also control "nonqualified" assets such as money obtained from inheritances or properties you may have sold. Even though these assets are nonqualified because they are not directly in your retirement fund, they are still part of the stash of cash from which you will live in the future.

Every asset you accumulate over the course of your lifetime should be viewed as continually flowing into a large pot of money from which you will draw your retirement income. That was my realization twenty years ago working with stocks and real estate portfolios. The ultimate goal of all our investments is to have a pot of money down the road that provides more income than our budget needs.

I always define "wealth" as having more money coming in from savings and investments when you retire than what's going out to pay your budget necessities—without having to work or receive Social Security or other assistance from family! The shame is that only 5 percent of Americans fall into this definition.

We have a lot of different things in our pot of money that we need to control and manage. Nowadays, 60 percent of that needed pot of money is no longer located in our employers' core retirement plans since, as we've seen, most of the core plans have been replaced by 401(k)s. As a result, our control and flexibility over our retirement money is reduced because 401(k)s are managed by somebody else. And that "somebody" is the Wall Street Casinos. Since you've read this far, you know that can't be good for you!

Let's take a quick moment to describe what I mean by control and flexibility over your savings and investments. Control is the ability to liquidate or refinance the asset WHEN you need it—not when or at the dictates of the market or economy! In other words, you have no control (and therefore no flexibility) over your savings or net worth if you don't know what the account or asset will be worth at a future time when needed or if you are unable to make a phone call and receive the funds in a timely manner.

If your money is "buried in your backyard" as real estate equity and you need cash fast for emergencies or income needs, you have to ask your banker for YOUR money—and then hope the economic climate isn't like the situation in 2008 or 2009 when you do so. Nothing is more upsetting than witnessing someone who was diligent in paying off all or most of their home who needs cash to pay bills when they lose a job, get disabled, or become sick and the lender says "Yeah, I know the money's buried in the backyard, but you can't qualify to pay it back!"

Also, good luck getting a sell order into your broker to get out of the stock market when it's in a freefall during a panic. The government can shut down the stock markets for a week to cool things down, and who knows what your stocks will be worth after it reopens.

Another vital aspect of controlling your money is this: Never invest in a limited partnership or any passive investment that limits your access to the money when you might need it or want out for a better opportunity. You may be giving money to people who may be unable to run a successful business venture or who have no control over economic variables like housing or energy recessions, high inflation, terrorism, or natural disasters. But they sure can give a good sales pitch about why you should invest with them and trust their ability to make you as much money as they'll make upfront off you. Moreover, when the company run by the general partners fails, you won't be able to get your money out because, as limited partner, you do not have liquidity or a say in the financial decisions that affect your money. For example, some real estate and oil and gas limited partnerships in the mid-1980s and early 1900s failed and drained their investors' money. And these were put together by huge Wall Street entities! The limited partners could do nothing but wait for the destruction to settle and see if there was anything left after the class action suits were filed. They got pennies on their hard-earned dollars. These investors weren't stupid people. They were doctors and lawyers and other professionals...who got taken for a ride on Wall Street.

The lesson I've sought to impart throughout this book is never relinquish control of your finances to other people. When you allow someone else to be in charge of your money, someone like a broker at a major Wall Street firm, you abdicate responsibility for your own future well-being. You need to call the shots on not only your 401(k) plan's investment decisions but also all your other assets because everything you have contributes to your retirement pot.

Remember that if you cannot make a call and receive your money in a timely manner when you need it, you have no control. If you are unable to tap the cash buried in your "backyard" or your rental properties for emergencies, you are not in control of your money—the bank is!

The Third Pillar: Market Gains, Not Losses

Now let's examine the third pillar of the Safe Money System: participation in long-term stock market performance without stock market risk.

Historically, the stock market will give us 8 to 10 percent annual returns over a period of fifteen to twenty years, not the 10-15 percent that the stock peddlers like to tout. Moreover, we don't know which periods of time will give us only 5 percent and which periods will give us 10 percent. We don't know when the next big storm will be that could wipe all our investments clean. These storms (defined as at least 30 percent declines) happened in 1972-1975, 1981-1984, the early '90s, 2000-2002, and recently in 2008-2009. Anyone with a lick of business common sense knows that cyclical storms interrupt periods of sustained growth in stocks or real estate, but no one can predict exactly when they will occur. No one but the Fed and the Wall Street bankers knows when the credit markets will dry up yet again, causing the "musical chair panic" called recession.

If we look more closely at the returns that investors received over the last decade or so, we will see that most are no better off than they were in 1996. Let's take a look at Cindy, who put some money into the stock market in 1996. She made 85 percent on her money from 1997 to 2000. Then she lost it all the growth and some of her principal with the 46 percent market decline during the tech bubble from 2000-2002. Wait a minute! How does a 46 percent loss wipe out my 85 percent gain? Well, her $100,000 in 1996 grew to $185,000 by early 2000. Then the 46 percent loss reduced her account value to $100,000—back to square one, if you will. Remember when I told you that stock losses hurt you more than gains help you?

She regained most of what she lost during 2003-2007 when the markets gained 65 percent, taking her account back to $165,000. Recently, though, in 2008-2009, Janet lost 35 percent as the over-bought real estate and stock market bubble burst. Now, not only has Janet lost all her gains, but this latest loss took her all the way back to her 1996 account value of around $100,000! It has been a lost thirteen years for Janet.

Had she used the Safe Money System, put her $100,000 into a guaranteed principal account, and only received 4 percent annually, she'd have $170,000 in her account. This is what my clients did, and they received more than 4 percent annually. As my clients look back over the last thirteen years, do you think they remember the huge gains from 1996-2000 or 2003-2007? No! But they know they slept well during the disasters in 2000-2003 and the last two years, knowing that their money was locked-in and safe!

When we are looking to invest in financial products, we have to examine things for the long haul. We have to ask questions like what is the average percent yield over a certain period of time after fees and commissions? In Cindy's case, the yield came out to zero or perhaps even negative over thirteen years. She might make back some of her money down the road and reclaim an average of 8 to 10 percent average annual return for her investment in stocks, but remember that an 8 percent annual gross yield is only 6 percent after the average annual mutual fund management and broker fees are deducted. A CD averaging 4-5 percent would have increased her money by 75 percent over thirteen years. A fixed index annuity would have given her a 7-8 percent annual gain (without management and broker fees) and more than doubled her money over thirteen years—without all the drama, worries, and headaches involved.

Therefore, the Safe Money System promotes products that won't fall short of stock market performance over the long run and, unlike stocks, will provide you with positive and stable returns even in a down stock market. How can that be? Keep reading!

The Fourth Pillar: Lock In Your Gains

The fourth and last Safe Money pillar centers on the lock-in mechanism that secures the growth of your account values to prevent losses during a future downturn. What's the use of having growth on your investment if sometime in the future we hit a down cycle? What's the use of accumulating all those assets when you could lose it all when the music stops, and you don't get to a chair in time? That is why I like products with a lock-in mechanism that secures the gains and ensure that nothing is lost from year to year.

Remember Cindy's bumpy ride with her $100,000 from 1996 to 2009? With the lock-in mechanism of the fixed index annuity, she would have not given up her market gains when the sharp declines hit. In fact, using real historic numbers of the S&P 500 index (the index in which Cindy would have participated), she would have doubled her money in thirteen years rather than breaking even with all the stress, and she was only participating in 65 to 70 percent of the market gains—but none of its losses!

Safe Money Strategies

After our discussion of the four pillars of a worry-free financial plan, I want to address some points to supplement your understanding of the Safe Money System.

I don't steer my clients into qualified retirement accounts like IRAs, 403(b)s, or 401(k)s—unless my client's company offers a match on my client's contributions into his/her retirement funds. In that case, I would say never exceed your company's contribution if the company has a policy that limits its own contribution. Why contribute more of your hard-earned money just for more risk? You should contribute just enough to get your company to put in its full share of its match—nothing more.

I personally don't own an IRA or other qualified retirement account—never have and never will! I don't like having an IRS tax lien on my future pot of money—a lien that could substantially decrease my share of the pot for lifetime income as tax rates rise over the next five to ten years. Where do you think tax rates will be after the additional trillions of dollars that have been thrown at the Wall Street firms, banks, Fannie Mae, and Freddie Mac to keep them afloat? Up? Down? The same?

You know the answer! We have to pay for this deficit mess at some time in the future not to mention funding the huge deficits in Social Security, Medicare, and the looming healthcare crisis! Serving that current $13 trillion debt (and growing) means that tax revenues must increase.

I don't want to have my retirement future held hostage by the IRS when I know that down the road the tax I'll pay will far surpass the benefit I received with my contributions and accumulations.

Let's use an illustration because numbers are your friend: A forty-five-year-old investor puts $10,000 into a supplemental retirement program his 403(b), Deferred Comp 457, or 401(k) plan after the employer match. He gets an 8 percent return a year for twenty years from the supplemental saving program. His employer and the government encourage him to do so because the core pension is likely going to be non-existent or at best inadequate to fund the retirement lifestyle equal in income to his working years.

The government gives you monetary incentives to put money into the supplemental program. The government says to you, "Put $10,000 in your retirement fund, and we're going to give you a $3,000 tax savings (assuming you are in a combined 30 percent federal and state tax bracket)." So it only costs you $7000 a year to contribute $10,000. Your accumulated tax savings from the government would come to $60,000 over those twenty years ($3000 per year x 20 years). That sounds really attractive at first, doesn't it? Well, there are multiple ways we can look at this situation that might change your mind.

After twenty years, if you get 8 percent annual returns on your contributions, you would have accumulated $450,000. When you're sixty-five, you'll have some decisions to make. You always had your eye on that second home out in Palm Desert or St. George, Utah. So you want to buy a house, and you cash in. To take your $450,000 out as income, you have to pay 42 percent in combined fed and state taxes. Before, you received a 30 percent tax benefit. Now taxes are higher because the lump sum distribution is ordinary income of $450,000 and thus a higher tax bracket. So $450,000 minus 42 percent of $450,000 is $261,000, which is what you actually have in cash to buy your vacation dream home. You just sent the government an $189,000 thank you in one lump payment for their $60,000 tax benefit over the last twenty years. You should ask yourself one question: Whose retirement plan was this after all—mine or Uncle Sam's?

In another scenario, your tax advisor would tell you to take money out "the smart way" over the course of twenty years in retirement rather than a lump sum of $450,000 because you'll be killed in taxes as seen in the previous paragraph. Well, you follow their advice and take out $50,000 annually from your retirement fund from age sixty-six to eighty-five. Now when you withdraw $50,000 annually as income, you get charged 30 percent in taxes because $50,000 (plus all your other Social Security and other income) puts you in the 30 percent combined tax category. So each year you are charged $15,000 in taxes. Over twenty years of payouts, your tax bite grew to $300,000 ($15,000 x 20 years), doing it the "smart way")! But your benefit from the government was still $60,000. Bad plan.

What is a better way to go? I tell people to pay the IRS its $3,000 a year while they're saving the $10,000 annually for twenty years and not take the government bait—I mean benefit. This way, your loss compared to the other scenarios is minimized. You only pay $60,000 in total taxes over the next twenty to forty years (age forty-five to eighty-five) instead of the much larger numbers in the above scenarios. Why does this make sense?

Well, originally our example showed that you have $10,000 to save per year. With my strategy, you gave $3,000 to the IRS, and now you have $7,000 to save for retirement. It's wiser to keep that $7,000 out of your supplemental retirement fund and choose between the following two Safe Money strategies:

Strategy A:

Put $7,000 annually into a structured life insurance contract under current IRS parameters that will act like a supercharged Roth account without the IRS's age and income restrictions as to accessibility before age fifty-nine and a half. The benefit is that the buildup of your savings is tax free, meaning that if your savings bring in 5 percent returns this year, this 5 percent will not be taxed.

Another benefit is that withdrawing your money out of the life insurance cash account for pre-retirement emergencies or needs can also be tax free using loans under current tax law. If you die prior to your desired retirement age, there is a tax-free death benefit for your loved ones that will be substantially more than the after-tax amount of your qualified account.

The math also shows that your monthly income from the life insurance contract would provide an additional 40 percent more monthly income than the traditional qualified plan due to the tax-free loan provisions of the life policy—40 percent more income plus an enhanced death benefit that qualified plans don't give you!

You are able to achieve a comparable 8 percent annual return to the mutual funds in your qualified plan on the cash value of the life policy by using the same indexing strategy I use in the fixed index annuity, including the lock-in of future account values as you near retirement—without the mutual fund risk exposure!

Strategy B:

Put that $7,000 into investment real estate where you would receive the same tax benefits from depreciation

and other expenses as contributing money to a qualified plan. However, you would get more control and flexibility over your money outside of the IRS's restrictions on qualified plans because you can refinance, sell, or hang on to the real estate property. If you have to choose between putting $1,000 in stocks or in real estate (with its leverage), it is better to put the money in real estate for the long haul. I would ask my clients to not give me $1000 to put into a qualified plan or IRA and instead put it in real estate. Ten years down the road, when a downturn happens, you can still sell or refinance your real estate to survive, whereas you would have no control over your stocks shrinking in value.

Your accountant will confirm my numbers on the above illustrations because math is math, and the tax laws are what they are. He or she will not give advice about investments or real estate because they cannot be sure which investments or property purchases are the best for you or what your parameters are. So it is up to you to figure out personal parameters that would affect your real estate decisions on your own, using my advice of seeking balance and contentment for you and your family. We will continue our discussion of real estate and establishing contentment in later chapters.

Currently, trillions of dollars are being thrown into the world economy for bailouts. Decades from now, Americans will likely be paying higher taxes to repay the cost of those bailouts. We need to be reminded that up till 1987, this country had marginal federal tax brackets as high as 70 percent—plus additional taxes in most states! That fact should get people scratching their heads and saying, "Tell us more about that," or "How did that happen, and will it happen again?" Remember earlier in the book? I explained the importance of your advisor understanding the taxes on your overall planning strategies under the Safe Money System.

The strategies that I have shown work to save you money within all of today's tax laws and give you an idea of how to look at the numbers if tomorrow's tax laws change. The numbers that I shared with you are real. You can't refute them, and you can't argue with them. You must find better investment and savings strategies like the Safe Money System to help you navigate the tax laws and in the end to be able to finance your retirement dreams.

Part II

The Safe Money System
Strategies for the Affluent

(and they work for the rest of us, too!)

The Miracle of Leverage, Compounding Interest, and Wealth Creation without Risk

Chapter 6

What the Heck Happened to Mike Tyson's Millions?

Sometimes people ask me, "Do the affluent really need the Safe Money System?" It's a fair question. Sure, these strategies seem like a great idea for anyone worried about losing their retirement funds. But what about those lucky people who have so much money it seems like they can weather any loss?

As a former professional baseball player, I've befriended some very wealthy people in my lifetime. I've known men and women with incredible net worth—professional athletes, entertainment celebrities, and titans of industry in the business world. After many years of observation, I've come to the realization that the wealthy are not immune to risk and loss. In fact in some ways, they're even more susceptible to it.

How many times do we read a story in the news about someone who made millions of dollars, then ended up broke? Look at Mike Tyson. He went from being king of the world to losing it all. Evander Holyfield, Burt Reynolds—I can think of dozens of people who have graced (or disgraced) the front pages of gossip magazines. They become the butt of jokes on late-night television, the hapless football star or the ruined celebrity. They didn't have parameters in place to keep their money safe, and they didn't have the foresight to take a part of their money and set it aside for guaranteed cash flow in the future, in case things got bad. When things *did* get bad, they had nothing to fall back on.

The majority of people, who get a windfall of cash, whether it's from career success, an inheritance, or winning the lottery, lose that money within five to ten years. Statistics show that 65-70 percent of professional athletes, entertainers, and musicians are in severe financial stress within three years of ending their career—if they're not dead broke.

How does it happen? These guys have whole teams of people working for them—agents, managers, accountants, and attorneys. So why aren't these so-called experts telling them how to keep their money safe? Where are the smart people on Wall Street telling them to put their money into Safe Money System strategies?

The answer is obvious: Wall Street doesn't want you to have access to these strategies. They want your money under control and management in vehicles that will keep kicking out commissions to them whether you make money or not. Most advisors to the affluent don't know about the Safe Money strategies, or they're afraid to give them to their clients. They don't have the parameters around their own lives on how they conduct business, and as a result, they don't advise their clients how to do safe things with their money.

And then there are people like Bernie Madoff, who prey on

the most affluent, and who burn through millions like dollar bills.

It's not just about bad investments—it's about the lifestyle. Many of the people who make a lot of money no longer have a moral compass. They feel invincible, like the party is never going to end. Then comes that fateful day when they realize that the party became more important then their relationship with their spouse, their kids, or their faith. Once their career is over, the party is, too.

That's when they look up and say, "I don't have anything. I don't have any money. I don't have any career. I don't have any self-esteem because it was based on how well I performed and how much money I made. And here I am. I got nothing."

The biggest enemy on the path to protecting your wealth and your happiness is ignorance. Being ignorant doesn't mean you're a bad person; it just means you don't have the knowledge and understanding you need. And if you don't have knowledge and understanding, you certainly can't have wisdom. Being wise means understanding how to take the knowledge behind ***The Safe Money System*** and apply it in this particular area of your life.

Unfortunately, nobody ever teaches us wisdom. It's not a course you can sign up for in high school or college. If it were, maybe all the Wall Street executives and real estate moguls wouldn't be losing millions!

The problem starts when you give up control. Let's say you got a hot tip from a friend or colleague and became a limited partner in a real estate LLC. You have no control over what happens with that property—when it's sold or re-financed. You poured money into it because somebody said, "Hey, so-and-so owns property and he's filthy rich. Why aren't you?" So you leapt without looking, and today you have no control over that money at all.

The only way to control your money is to understand what it's doing. What's the risk? What's the worst-case scenario? You also need a minimal expectation of where you should be ten, fifteen, twenty years down the road. That's the bare minimum. If it's better than that, it's gravy on the taters.

When your money's with the Wall Street casino, you don't have an answer to these questions. You have no control. So there's a lack of understanding coupled with a lack of control—a dangerous cocktail.

Then there's that pesky little thing I call "ego." Most people I know who made a lot of money and lost it have incredible egos. When their buddies said "How come you're not manning up and getting in on this deal?", they couldn't bear to miss out on the action. Not only did they not have the courage to say no; they didn't have the pre-established boundaries that would allow them to say, "That doesn't fit into the boundaries and parameters of what I'm doing with my money or my life."

The world of entertainment and sports are a scary place to grow old—they're always looking for the young. Sadly, I can count on one hand the professional baseball players I knew who sat down at thirty and said, "At fifty, I'm not going to be able to throw a fastball the way I can now. I need some good wisdom counseling to figure out how to preserve my fortune and my family."

When I look at these people, I see a gaping hole when it comes to their life purpose. Someone with life purpose says, "I am getting old, and yes, I'm continually heading toward that curtain called death. But I am purposed to be the biggest blessing to everybody around me." These people are happy, because they're on **Purpose**. They have happy marriages because they **purpose** to have a happy marriage. They're good parents because they **purpose** to raise their kids with love and wisdom. They're good businessmen because they **purpose** to grow a fair, strong business. The fruit of that purpose is happiness. Not that it's always going to be easy street; a lot of happiness is born out of challenges. But you've got to have purpose along the way.

A lot of people today are completely dependent on performance for their happiness. Their self-esteem is all wrapped up in the accumulation of things and how well they do their job—playing sports, writing music, and making movies. But it's all scoreboard… bank balances. And scoreboard is not **purpose**.

Scoreboard is just activity.

When I counsel professional athletes and entertainers, I'm always amazed that they rarely have parameters or boundaries set up. They might make $5 million a year and give $2 million to the government in taxes. Beyond that, they don't have a whole lot of boundaries when it comes to the remaining $3 million. So, I sit down with them and we work out a way to make that money last. To ensure that they can take care of themselves, their future and their family. We set up a system so that they know that money will be there down the road when their throwing arm, singing voice, or young skin unfortunately exits the building.

I don't care if you come in with $50,000 or $5 million: there's a part of that money that you've earned the right to have fun with. That's probably 10 to 25 percent. But there's also a part of that money that you can't afford to lose. I recommend putting the other 75-80 percent away for your future. That way, you can continue to have fun down the road instead of being the brunt of jokes about how greedy and stupid you were not to take care of your future when you were given a golden opportunity to do so.

Do the affluent need ***The Safe Money System***?

Of course they do. No matter how much money we make, we all have money we can't afford to lose. And we all need strategies for safekeeping, strategies that affect not just our money but our lives.

So let's talk about Safe Money strategies for the wealthy—and for the rest of us, too. In the following chapters, I'm going to walk you through several new strategies using investment vehicles we haven't discussed, Primarily: life insurance.

Chapter 7

LIFE INSURANCE: The Misconceptions and the Truth that Wall Street is Hiding from You

Before we talk about life insurance, let's review the Four Pillars of ***The Safe Money System.***

1) Guarantee the safety of your principal
2) Control and flexibility of your money
3) A crediting method for growth on your money based on participation in the stock market gains, but not the losses
4) A lock-in mechanism that secures the growth of your account value to prevent losses during a future downturn.

So far in this book, we've mostly talked about the use of fixed-guaranteed annuities to secure your retirement future. Annuities are the darlings of the Four Pillars. And yet, if you work with Wall Street brokers or have a lot of money, I'll bet you've gotten an earful about why you don't want or need annuities, and why these vehicles aren't right for you.

I'm here to tell you...some of those reasons are valid.

Annuities are great investment vehicles, *when you need income.* And when $500,000 is the last dime you have to your name and you're laid off at fifty-five years old, income is exactly what you need. Or maybe you've got $1 million at age sixty-five in your pension plan, and that's it, Charlie. You might have made $100,000 a year, but now you've got to figure out how to take that $1 million, not lose a penny of it, and make it last for the next twenty years. How are you going to maintain the same annual income you had when you retired? Mathematically, it ain't gonna happen. Especially not if you lose any principle along the way.

If you have $1 million in retirement funds and you're getting 5 percent annually, that means you'll get around $75,000 a year for twenty years. What happens if that money is subject to Wall Street risk? What if the value goes down by 50 percent like it has **TWICE** in the last ten years? How long will that money last you then?

The answer is: not very. That's why a fixed annuity that guarantees you a set income can be a very good idea.

But most wealthy people fall into a different category. A person who's got $10 million doesn't need income; they need to hang on to the $10 million. So they come to me and say, "Why do I want an annuity? First of all, I don't need income. And second, my accountant told me I want to stay in stocks and bonds and real estate, because then when I die, my heirs will get the money with the stepped-up basis." (The stepped-up basis means that all of the capital gains on those assets that were in stocks, bonds, mutual funds, securities, and real estate are eliminated and the present value to the heirs is stepped up at the person's death.)

In an annuity, the money has been tax-deferred during the growth stage. That means that my clients with annuities have made, on average, 6 to 8 percent over the last twenty years. While that money is growing, it might double every twelve years. And if you hold an annuity that has deferred growth in it, that becomes ordinary income to the heirs. We might be talking $100,000 or $1 million, but regardless, that's not a good deal. Ordinary income is taxed as high as 42 percent, state and federal. This is why financial planners to the affluent often do not recommend annuities to their clients—because their heirs will pay a formidable price for that money.

While annuities can be fantastic vehicles for qualified retirement plans (because you're not going to spend that money; it's meant for income), they may not be the best place for your non-qualified funds. Non-qualified funds, remember, include all the money that is not in those qualified plans (IRA, 401k, etc.). It's the post-taxed money that's in the bank, the stock market, CDs, treasuries—wherever it is. So why would you want to put that liquid money into something that's going to have a non-stepped-up situation, leaving your estate vulnerable to getting clobbered with taxes?

This is the question foremost on the minds of my affluent clients. They want to know: If annuities aren't going to cut it, have you got something else for me?

As a matter of fact, I do.

Strategy #1:

Single-Pay Life Insurance – It's time has come!

My clients have been using this strategy for years, to great success. In many ways, a single-pay life insurance policy acts like an annuity: it grows tax-deferred. But here's what happens that makes it different.

Most of the time my clients don't touch their single-pay life insurance policies because they don't need income; they have other money. But unlike an annuity, these policies enable them to leverage a tax-free death benefit. This benefit goes to their estate or to their heirs, eliminating the objection that the money gets taxed heavily when they pass on. In fact it's even *better* than a stepped-up basis.

It's a stepped-up basis ***plus additional money in tax-free life insurance*** that you don't have with stocks and bonds.

More importantly, stocks and bonds don't give you any protection of principal. A single-pay **Index Universal Life** insurance program, on the other hand, is flexible, while giving you guaranteed principle, stock market growth without stock market risk, and a locked-in mechanism. Go ahead and check off every one of those Four Pillars with a check plus!

Another feature of the single-pay Index Universal Life insurance is you're your participation of the stock market growth the internal interest credits are about 2.5 times higher than what an annuity pays, meaning the caps are higher on how much you can make. Currently, you can participate in a single-pay life insurance policy and receive an annual return of caps of the S&P index, the Dow, the NASDAQ, the London Exchange—whatever index you want to track and participate in. Your money is not at risk; you're just getting a participation of the growth without the risk.

Most single-pay life insurance policies capture as high as 12-15 percent of that stock index return in that year. If the market did 25, you can make 12-15. If it did 10, you get all of the 10. If it did 20, you might get 12-15 of the 20 ... at no risk to you.

Compare this to most annuities, where you're looking at getting around 6-7 percent. Why? Because most people are not going to keep their money in annuities as long as they would in life insurance. They'll typically tap it for income. The insurance companies don't have the money long enough to make money on your money, so they can't pay you as high a participation rate. With life insurance, it's a longer hold for the insurance companies, so you get to participate with them in the process.

Simply put, they stand to gain more from your money, so they're willing to give you a bigger share of the winnings.

In summary, a single-pay life insurance policy gives you the gift of accumulation. Like an annuity, you have no risk of principle, and you get a higher participation of stock index. You have as much flexibility, if not more, and you don't lose the stepped-up basis that you get with your stocks and bonds.

You now have a tax-free benefit that can be as much as 50 percent higher than what you've actually got in the cash value.

Now that's a pretty good deal for your heirs!

Sorry, Wall Street. You want to object that life insurance can't be a good vehicle for creating and maintaining wealth? **Objection overruled.**

Strategy #2:

Creating Wealth for ages 30-50

Using Life Insurance to Create a Tax-Free Retirement

Did I get your attention with tax-free retirement? I should hope so!

I stated in Chapter 3 why I recommend the use of a properly structured Universal Index Life policy to fund your retirement, but it bears repeating.

You want to accumulate tax-free, borrow out income tax-free, and have a leveraged higher cash benefit for your family tax-free.

If you are under age 50 and currently contributing to an unmatched 401(k) or IRA, you need to have your financial advisor do a long term comparison of between funding your retirement with stocks or mutual funds (uncertainty of performance and risk) to a Universal Index Life Policy. You'll be more than shocked at how well the life insurance measures up and surpasses the Wall Street Casino method of retirement planning.

The truth is that it's impossible to know where we'll be in five or ten or twenty years when it comes to taxes. Current tax laws are certainly in flux, and who knows where the estate tax, estate planning tax, or the income tax will end up? One thing we know for darn sure: they're not going to be lower. You don't solve the problem of a $14.5 trillion deficit by lowering the revenues that the country takes in. We're going to have to pay the piper for a lot of stupid decisions the government has made over the last twenty-five years. And I'm not pointing fingers across party lines—I mean Democrats and Republicans alike.

If tax laws are going to be higher down the road—and believe me, they will be—you want to take advantage of anything that's going to give you tax-free income.

Currently, you get tax-free income from things like a Roth IRA. A Roth IRA is a nice vehicle, but in order to get one, you have to take your money out of your existing normal IRA, get taxed on it, and then convert it over so that the growth from that point forward will come out tax-free. But here's where the danger lies: they can change the rules at anytime. I call it "**future tax-law risk**."

They might decide, for example, that it will no longer be fifty-nine and a half when you can access your Roth. Maybe now you'll have to wait until you're sixty-five. Can they do that? Sure they can. They can also limit how much you're allowed to put into it. If you're under fifty, you can only put in $5,000 a year. If you're over fifty, you can put in $6,000 a year. What if you've got more than that? Tough luck—you've been restricted.

This is why I advise people to use life insurance to create a tax-free retirement. How?

By taking a lump sum of money that's not in your qualified plan, and repositioning that money into an **Index Universal Life Insurance** policy with a series of annual deposits. If you're under fifty, you do it with four annual deposits. If you're over fifty, you do it with five.

Let's say you have $1 million. If you're forty-eight, you put $250,000 into this type of policy each year, for the next four years. The reason you're doing this is that the IRS is requiring you to do it in order to create a tax-free loan provision. Down the road, you can withdraw the accumulation on that money, tax-free.

Plus you'll now have created a higher benefit than the cash value—income tax free—to your heirs.

Remember: you're doing this for your income—the income tax-free death benefit is just "gravy on the taters"!

Maybe you have $5-10,000,000 to your name, and you want to start earmarking some of that money for future income needs. This is the money you've identified **that you don't want to lose**. You need it down the road, in case things don't work out in your business ventures. This is not the money you get to play with; this is serious money. This goes in the "I can't afford to not have this in my future" pot.

We talked about the power of indexing in an earlier chapter, and how it exercises the Four Pillars of ***The Safe Money System***. This same principle is true when it comes to life insurance. The crediting of the cash is using the same strategy. The good news about this vehicle is that you can access the money anytime. It's not a retirement plan; you don't have to wait until you're a certain age like you do with qualified plans or annuities. The downside to those vehicles is that you get taxed on the money that comes out before you reach a certain age. Because the life insurance policy is a tax-free loan, there are no restrictions. No tax. No age requirement. No strings attached

You may be asking yourself, "What if they change the tax laws regarding tax-free loans in ten or fifteen years?" Great question—I'm glad you asked.

There's a rule in the US Constitution that has to do with contractual law called the **Ex Post Facto** provision. That's Latin for "**nothing after the fact**." Never in the history of our country has

Congress come along and changed an existing constitutional provision that would affect past business contracts.

Instead, they say, "Everything up to this point is grandfathered under past law. From this point forward, it changes." What that means for you: if you've already established a life insurance contract, then you're grandfathered in.

I'm not saying they won't change it or can't change it. I'm saying it's not very likely because of that **Ex Post Facto** rule.

Another reason I like to use life insurance is that it makes great emergency money. If the last five years have taught us anything, it's to be prepared. I don't care how much money you've got: life happens. If you're breathing air, you're probably subject to some financial stress and uncertainty. Maybe your grandkids can no longer afford to go to college, because your kids lost their money in the stock market. And here you are, retired, with this money. How great would it be to go into a tax-free loan to help fund your grandkids' education?

I call that "family banking." Family banking gives you the opportunity to use your money to help your family, rather than having your money under the control of the bank or buried in real estate.

Remember what I've been saying throughout this book: if you're truly going to have a Safe Money System, ***you*** have to be the one in control, not anybody else. With tax rates most likely on the rise, a tax-free strategy is the right strategy to have.

Strategy #3:

Tax-Deductible Life Insurance

"What?" you're saying. "Tax-deductible dollars? I was told I couldn't buy life insurance inside a qualified plan!"

The secret to this strategy—buying life insurance with tax-deductible dollars you already have in your plan—is in the source of how the premium payments are made.

Let's review how it works. We'll say you have a 401(k) with $1 million in it. You've just turned fifty-nine and a half (happy half birthday), so you are able to do a transfer into your IRA called an "**in-service, non-hardship distribution**" (more on that in the next chapter). Ninety-five percent of the plans out there, including government-deferred compensation plans, can be transferred into an IRA or another Qualified plan vehicle (Solo 401(k), Self-Employed IRA or SEP, etc). We talked about this in Chapter 3 — how to continue to work at your job while moving your money to a place where ***you*** control the investment of your assets, rather than leaving it in a 401(k) where you have minimal control. The IRS is not concerned because it's only a temporary tax-free transfer; but they're going to get their pound of flesh a little later down the road.

But here's what you can do in a solo 401(k) that you can't do in an IRA or a 401(k). **You can take 25 percent of your assets and purchase a life insurance policy with it.** So you have $1 million and you do an ***in-service distribution***, or you've retired. You take that 401(k) and move it to a solo 401(k). Most of you who have that kind of money aren't really retiring; you're still doing some sort of consulting work. So you take out $250,000, and you put the remaining $750,000 into a fixed index annuity that's going to begin to get interest crediting and grow. You'll probably get a guarantee on that account, and you'll use that for income down the road as needed.

With the $250,000, you're going to buy a single-pay life insurance policy. As I explained in **Strategy #1**, you're going to be able to buy a leveraged amount of death benefit ("leveraged" meaning **more** than what you put into it). So if you put $250,000 into a life insurance policy, you'll more than likely get $500,000+ of death benefits, income tax-free. The $250,000 is the cash value part of it, but if you die, there's an extra amount of money that will be created.

What happens is that, in this case, you've used tax-deductible dollars. You don't pay any additional premiums, and you're sitting there with a life insurance policy that at your death will pay out probably two or three times what you put into it. **That's tax-free money to your beneficiaries**! All you have to put back into the solo 401(k) is the original $250,000 premium you started with. Everything else gets to stay with the estate — income tax-free!

Strategy #4:

Funding Your Retirement by Buying Your Parents a Life Policy

When I was forty-four years old and my mom was sixty-three, I bought a life insurance policy for several hundred thousand dollars on my mom's life. For the last fifteen years, I've paid for that policy. **It hasn't cost her a cent.**

Why did I do that? Because I figured out that between age sixty-three and eight-five (which was my mother's life expectancy),

I would pay about $80,000 into that policy. And while there's no way to know for certain which of us will pass on to the other side of the curtain first, more than likely, my mother will go before I will. When she passes, I will get a tax-free benefit of over $300,000 for my family. That's a tax-free benefit.

The $80,000 I spent along the way is part of my retirement plan. At forty-four, I knew that I'd be working for the next twenty-five years. I sat down with my mom and said, "How would you like to make sure that I have some money for my retirement without costing you a dime? And I promise not to kill you!"

She laughed and said, "Of course!" It was an easy way for her to help enhance the retirement planning for my family and I, without costing her a dime.

The wealthiest parents in the world already have life insurance policies. The Gates and the Rockefellers—they're already using these strategies. They've had life insurance policies their whole lives. But many parents don't, and it's a great way to bolster **your** retirement plan without costing **them** any additional money. And they're usually fine with it ... as long as they trust you not to knock 'em off!

I'm half joking, of course. But in all seriousness, the trust factor is important. Before you broach this idea with your parents, make sure they know that you genuinely have their best interest and well-being at heart.

You can use the insurability of your parents to fund your retirement, or set up a college fund for your children, their grandchildren. It may seem like a hefty investment, but when you look at what it costs to buy the life insurance, compared to the tax-free benefits, you'll see why it's worth it.

When my mom passes on, I'll get over $300,000 of income tax-free death benefits that's equal to about $550,000 — if it were in my IRA. In order to make this same return on Wall Street, I'd have to be guaranteed 15 percent a year. Good luck getting 10 percent consistently with Wall Street!

So you now have some ways to make the most of the dollars in your non-Qualified plan using life insurance.

Great!

Next I want to talk about how to put the funds in your Qualified Plans to work. That money isn't lost to you. In fact, with the right Safe Money strategies, you can make it more profitable than you ever imagined.

Chapter 8

Taking Control of the Dollars in your Qualified Plan

If you read Chapter 3, you know my general feeling about Qualified Plans. I have a strong belief that they aren't necessarily going to get you where you want to go. The primary reason is that, as long as the IRS controls the Qualified Plan—i.e., your IRA, 403(b), 401(k), deferred comp, or Thrift Savings Plan (TSP)— they are essentially holding that money hostage. You can't get at it until you're fifty-nine and a half (or whatever age they decide). And if you try to tap into it before then, you'll be charged additional 10 percent federal plus state penalties for early withdrawal—or possibly more at some unknown tax rate in the future.

You really are held hostage to a future of unknowns. Right now, most people are receiving a tax savings at a rate of 15-25 percent on federal tax for their Qualified Plans.

But is that what the rate's going to be when you start taking it out?

I asked you this question in Chapter 3, and I'm going to ask it again: Where do you think tax rates will go with a current $14.5 trillion federal deficit and no political plan in place to solve it?

You guessed it: **UP!** There's just nowhere else for them to go!

Remember those Fram Oil Filter commercials? The tagline was, "Either pay me now or pay me later." You either pay the cost of a filter now, or you pay the cost of a whole freakin' engine later, when your motor seizes because you didn't do the maintenance on your car.

That's exactly what's happening in the current financial crisis. No one can pay now, so the government is going to make us pay later. The IRS can change the rules anytime they want. Like I said in the last chapter, they can raise the age from fifty-nine and a half to sixty-two or sixty-five. They can change the tax brackets; if you're getting a 15-25 percent benefit, they can turn around and make it like it was in the 1980s, when you had up to 70 percent in marginal federal tax brackets.

You think they can't do that? Just watch 'em!

So let's talk about some ways to take control of the money in your Qualified Plans. There are different options available to you, depending on if you're still working or not and how old you are. If you've still got your nose to the grindstone, how do you protect yourself from the Wall Street casino as you accumulate money?

Strategies to Protect your Retirement Assets before Retirement

The people who are still working fall into two groups: those under fifty-nine and a half, and those over. I'll start by addressing the first group.

If you're under fifty-nine and a half and working, and you're still contributing to your retirement accounts, either a 401(k) or another plan, it's imperative that you don't lose any money. But it's tricky because you're stuck with the mutual fund custodian that the company plan has contacted to manage your money — usually one of the large Wall Street custodians. Ten or fifteen years ago, people didn't give that much thought. After 2008, much thought!

If you're over fifty, you really can't afford to lose any money because your working years are numbered. At worst, your qualified money should be in what's called a "balanced" or "blended" mutual fund with stocks and bonds, reducing your risk (in theory) to big corrections in the stock market.

At best, if you're going to retire before age sixty, you need to be in short-term, high-grade corporate or government bonds, because you can't afford to lose any principal.

Corporate or government bonds help you take a little bit more control of the risk, rather than listening to the custodian's clerks tell you, "Oh, the market always comes back. Go ahead and stay fully invested." Keep in mind that the custodians make the most money when you're fully invested in the stock market and they're netting a juicy income off the annual fees. Those fees are not nearly as high if you're in corporate bonds, and they're even smaller when your money's in a money market account or government bonds.

So that's my advice for the under fifty-nine and a half set.

Now let's talk about if **you're still working and you're fifty-nine and a half** or older. What flexibility do you have to take control of your money in your 401(k), your government TSP, or your teacher's 403(b)?

The answer is: more than you've been told!

Over the last ten years we've had two **50 percent drops** in the stock market: between 2000 and 2003, and from late 2007 to early 2009. As we all know, it devastated people's retirement planning nationwide. There were people who were fifty-nine and a half and had planned to retire in the next five to ten years; now they can't. They saw their 401(k)s become 201(k)s in the blink of an eye.

What could they have done, if they'd know about it?

Three words, two hyphens. It's called an "**in-service, non-hardship distribution**".

Remember these words! It will protect your financial future!

In 2006, Congress introduced and endorsed this distribution for those employees who were over 59½, still working and who wanted to protect their retirement assets from the Wall Street Casino.

Simply put, it means you can go to your company's plan administrator and say, "How much of my 401(k) or Thrift Savings Plan (Deferred Comp) can I roll over to an IRA and keep working at this company?"

What few of you know is that 90 percent of corporations in the United States allow this. They by law have to tell you how much you can transfer and give you a form with which to do so. You are then allowed to take that money and do a tax-free transfer to an IRA where you now take control of that money with a Safe Money strategy.

That's great news for you!

It means you can take that money that was previously held hostage in the Casino and buy the savings vehicles that I've proposed in this book, like fixed-index annuities. You can do a self-directed IRA and pay cash for income-producing real estate. It can't be primary real estate or your primary home, but rental property? Sure. With that self-directed IRA, you can also buy mortgage notes and trust deeds; you can loan money out or buy existing notes or tax liens. Of course you need to discuss these strategies with your financial planner, but they're there and available to you. They exist in Congressional acts that became part of the IRS code for your benefit and protection—and control.

Now let's talk about the people who change jobs.

You've been laid off, quit, or retired. Let's say you have money in a 401(k). You don't need that ***in-service, non-hardship distribution***, because you are no longer "in service" now that you aren't working for the company. It might be a scary time for you personally, but the upside is that you have full control to take that 401(k) (or 403(b) or TSP) and roll it over to your own IRA where you can start using my Safe Money System strategies. You can even go get a new job and start contributing to the new 401(k) plan with new money that comes out of your paycheck.

But that old money can be pulled out of the Wall Street casino and put it in safe place, allowing you to build up your own retirement future without the casino's risk.

Then there's the people are who are under fifty-nine and a half and still working, but who need to get out their retirement money for **hardship reasons**. We've been talking about ***non*-hardship distributions**; but what if you have a hardship and you need to get that money? Maybe you need extra income, or there was another investment opportunity, or it helped pay for your mortgage—it could be any number of reasons.

I've got good news for you, too. There's a provision in the IRS tax code called Section 72T that allows you to take money out of your retirement account systematically over time. The stipulation? You have to do it for at least five years, *or* until you're fifty-nine and a half.

Let's say you're fifty-three years old. You've got $500,000 in your IRA and you need to get some money out of it, but you don't want to pay the 10 percent early withdrawal penalty to the federal government and whatever the additional penalty is in your state. So what you can do under **IRS Code 72T** is determine what your life expectancy is—if you're fifty-three, it's thirty-two years—and take out, over the next six and a half years, an amount of money subject to your life expectancy that will not be penalized, but will be taxed.

Once you reach fifty-nine and a half, you're done—you can stop taking the money out, or take more money out, or do whatever you want to do. But for those six and a half years, you can systematically take money out every year to meet your needs.

If you're fifty-six years old, you have to do it for three and a half years before you're fifty-nine and a half. You either have to do it until you're fifty nine and a half, or for a minimum of five years.

If you're in a situation where you need money out of your retirement account, talk it over with your financial advisor. These are just a few of the options available to you.

Legacy Planning

The last way I help people take control of the money in their Qualified Plan is through **Legacy Planning**. In other words, planning for the kids and grandkids, or your favorite charity. Your legacy is what you leave behind when you depart to the other side of the curtain. It's the way you enrich the lives of the people or institutions you love the most.

You've heard about some of the ways to do this, like a stretch or multi-generational IRA. That's where, at your death, your beneficiaries elect to stretch out the payments of the IRA over their life expectancy, to avoid the big tax hit they would incur if they took it all out in a lump sum as ordinary income. If you have $500,000 in your qualified plan and your spouse is a beneficiary, you can often do a spousal IRA where that money gets transferred over directly to their social security number, without being taxed, and they do with it as they see fit. But if your spouse is deceased and the money goes to your kids or your estate, they have to pay ordinary income tax on that money...unless they elect to stretch out the taxability with a Stretch IRA.

Multi-generational or Stretch IRAs are very popular now, but when my clients tell me they're thinking about it, I ask them the following question: If you're seventy-five and you have a qualified plan, and there's $500,000 to $1 million in this qualified plan, and your beneficiaries are in their fifties...do you really think that they want to take that money over the next thirty-five years? Different strokes for different folks, but my guess is: **no, they don't**!

It's like winning the lottery. If I win $10 million with a scratch-off card and they tell me, "Okay, you can have $10 million paid over twenty years, or you can have $5 million paid right now," I'm going to take that money now. That way I can manage it and set up my own income so I'm not subject to someone else's rules (not to mention highly volatile economic conditions) for the next twenty years.

So what's an alternative to a Stretch IRA?

Let's say you're over age seventy and you don't need that qualified money for income (but the IRS forces you to do so with the

Required Minimum Distribution (RMD) starting at age 70 1/2. You used the Safe Money strategies to put your money in fixed annuities and life insurance, and you're planning on leaving most of that $500,000 to your kids.

Why not take a five- to ten-year payout and buy a life insurance policy for your kids and grandkids?

This lets you leverage the money in your qualified plan. You get far more money, income tax free, because you were taking money out each year, paying taxes on it, and using the difference to buy a life insurance policy. There will be a big tax-free death benefit to your estate, and you can fund the college education of your grandkids, becoming a huge blessing to your family. This is a lot better than leaving it in a qualified plan that's going to get decimated by taxes down the road.

There's one more Safe Money strategy for Legacy Planning that I call the "**gifting strategy**." For this strategy, you actually take that money out, pay the tax, then systematically take the balance and gift it. Under current tax law, you are allowed to give $13,000 to each member of your family annually, and your spouse is allowed to do the same. You do the math—between your kids and grandkids, that's a lot of money you could be gifting each year!

Plus, you and your spouse are allowed to give $1,000,000 each over your lifetimes (as of the August 2011 time of this revision).

Many of my clients gift a set amount of money to their kids and grandkids each year to fund an Irrevocable Life Insurance Trust (ILIT) so that the death benefit is outside of their estate, not subject to estate taxes that would be due under current tax law if they have an estate over $5 million ($10 million for the couple). Their kids and grandkids will grieve them when they're gone, but they'll also be forever grateful for this incredible gift.

In these strategies, my clients' legacy lives on to continue to bless their heirs!

If any of these ideas interest you, I strongly suggest you make an appointment with the financial planner who gave you this book to discuss them further. My goal is to give you concepts and ideas, to show you a world where you can protect your retirement funds with creativity and flexibility. I encourage you to take these ideas back to your planner and see how they fit into your personalized retirement plan.

I wrote ***The Safe Money System*** is to give you more control. I want to arm you with more knowledge, which in turn gives you more understanding, which in turn gives you the financial wisdom you need to make the best decisions.

And that's a winning combination, whether you're affluent or not!

Part III

How the The Safe Money System Will Secure Your Financial Future

Chapter 9

Success Stories

There's a reason why some folks do not open their quarterly statements: The fear of seeing negative numbers on a page all started for them during that 20 percent stock market drop in July and August of 2008. When the drop occurred, people began asking, "What about that Safe Money thing I heard about? Maybe it's time I do myself a favor, and grab a lifeboat before the Wall Street ship sinks." Those who were smart enough to consider this visited us, and the rest was history.

After the July/August 2007 fiasco, things only got worse for the next two years; the S&P Index would drop another 40 percent. Yet, ***The Safe Money System's*** clients weren't feeling the loss one bit. From 2007 to 2009, many of my clients had account statements that showed an increase of 10 to 15 percent on their money without any decrease in principal. This increase included the bonus that insurance companies gave them from signing up for the annuities that I recommended.

During the last two years, I would ask my clients, "Are you feeling pretty good about making money while protecting money?"

And they would answer, "I have $550k in my retirement account now. Had I kept my money in a mutual fund, I would have $370k today. So, yeah, I'm feeling really good!"

None of them had any losses on their retirement accounts over the last ten years! My clients followed my strategy of transferring money out of stocks and mutual funds into the safety of CDs and annuities and my advice to extract money from their houses in the forms of mortgages, home equity loans, and reverse mortgages to create liquidity. I showed them how to take advantage of the arbitrage system by taking out a mortgage at one rate of interest, investing the money to earn a higher rate of returns, and earning the difference. As a result, if they ever come across an emergency like a job layoff or disability, they will have money in their pockets to take care of it. They won't have to go to the bank and beg to borrow their own money because the banker doesn't think they can repay it.

I also deterred my clients from making bad decisions for their retirement funds. If someone was tempted to buy a house in foreclosure down the street for a quick "fix & flip" as seen on TV, I told them, "Don't do it." The reason why is that my client needed to keep money liquid and not put it into a risky investment. I teach my clients to keep 20 to 30 percent of their money liquid in CDs or government bonds so they can handle any unforeseen issues in their lives. If that client had put his retirement money into buying another home without the knowledge, understanding, and control necessary to survive an overheated real estate market, he would have thrown money away and reduced his life expectancy from the ensuing stress. In the following, I'd like to share with you some stories about the success my clients achieved with ***The Safe Money System***.

The Texas Belle

In May of 2010, I received a phone call from a sixty-one-year-old woman in a large city in Texas. A friend of hers had heard about ***The Safe Money System*** on the radio and highly recommended it, so she promptly bought it on Amazon.

After our initial discussion, I requested that she fax me her financial statements so that I could review them and generate some ideas before our follow-up phone conference. I was a little blown away when the statements showed $575,000 in Qualified Retirement Plan assets—and she was 100 percent exposed to stock market risk!

After reading the book, she wanted to be safe with her "can't afford to lose" funds. So at the end of the month, I flew to Texas to meet with her in person. Because I'm licensed in Texas, I was able to help her transfer $475,000 of her funds into several fixed index annuities. I suggested she keep $100,000 in an IRA at her bank for immediate liquidity needs.

Today the woman is very pleased with her significantly reduced risk, and happy to know she will have an income throughout her retirement. And I was very pleased that this savvy lady was smart enough to place that call!

My Wife's Clever Girlfriend

In June of last year, my wife Crystal was out with several girlfriends celebrating our son's high school graduation. Though her friends knew me, they weren't familiar with what I do for a living. Crystal explained that I'd recently written a book about safe money investing, and one of the women's ears perked up. She explained to my wife that she had recently been laid off from her job and had lost over 35 percent of her money between 2008 and 2009. She asked for a copy of the book, and Crystal dropped one on her doorstep the next day.

The following week, she called, and I set up an appointment for her and her husband to come in. She had already read ***The Safe Money System***, and I asked her husband to read just the first two chapters of the book, which he did. When they came into the office, they brought their 401(k) and IRA statements with them, and we talked about the available options.

The woman, who is under fifty and separated from service, had an account that was fully exposed to stock mutual funds. After we talked, she decided to transfer her money into the fixed index annuities I'd mentioned in the book. Her husband decided to move his IRA to safety as well.

In the end? They transferred over $600,000 of assets that are no longer exposed to the Wall Street Casino.

My wife doesn't know an annuity from a pair of Jimmy Choo pumps—but thanks to her, their money is now safe!

The Shrewd Airline Captain

In October, I received a phone call from one of my oldest childhood friends, a pilot who flies for a major airline between the East Coast and Honolulu. He had walked into the cockpit and found his co-pilot reading ***The Safe Money System***. He saw my picture and name on the cover, grabbed the book, and said, "I grew up with this guy!"

The co-pilot said, "I heard a radio interview with Randy in Hawaii, and I ordered it on Amazon. Now go get your own copy so I can have my book back!"

So my friend bought a copy on Amazon and gave me a call once he'd finished reading. He had nearly a million dollars in his 401(k), and he was fed up with gambling in the Wall Street casino. He had just turned sixty and was starting to think pretty seriously about his retirement future. After several phone conversations about possible strategies, he asked me to meet him for dinner during a layover in Los Angeles. We caught up, had some laughs, and ultimately transferred over $900,000 (In Service Distribution) to several IRAs with fixed index annuity policies.

"I just can't believe it," my friend said, laughing. "I didn't know you could read, let alone write a book! I just knew you had a great fastball in high school, and that you frequently fell asleep during Shakespeare lectures in English class."

I grinned. "I just helped you protect nine hundred grand," I said. "Bet you Will Shakespeare couldn't do *that*!"

The Circumspect Ex-NBA Coach/Executive

I recently received an email from a retired NBA Coach/Executive with over twenty-five years NBA experience. He had heard me on my radio show in Phoenix, another city where I am licensed. After reading ***The Safe Money System***, he wanted me to help him with his pension planning. I reviewed his statements and saw that there was over $850,000 in IRA assets exposed to stock market risk.

After several phone conferences where we went over various strategies and the company's annuity policies, I drove to Phoenix to meet him. The result? I had him put about 25% of his money into CDs for liquidity. Then, I repositioned the rest of the assets into three different annuities, designed to provide immediate income for the next five years, then for years six through ten. After year ten, he'd have lots of options with the last annuity ladder.

Slam dunk!

Four Strategies for Successful Relationship Building

So how do the relationships between clients of ***The Safe Money System*** differ from what goes on in the Wall Street casino? I'm glad you asked! I have designed four strategies for Client Relationship Management that made the success stories that you just read possible. They are *Education*, *Evaluation*, *Implementation*, and *Preservation*.

Let's first discuss **Education**. My clients found me; I didn't hunt them down. They attended an educational workshop, visited our website, read about me in an interview in the media, or were referred to me by satisfied clients. ***The Safe Money System*** and the fundamental beliefs of our company resonated in their hearts. So in the first stage of my relationship with my client, I educate them about safe investments and about the system of risk on Wall Street.

The second stage is the **Evaluation** of the client's investment goals, parameters, and their lives in a broader sense. I want to help people discover a personalized strategy for their money that fits in with their goals and values. For example, a father makes $200,000 a year and is highly taxed. He has to figure out how to put four kids through college in the future, including giving them the option of going to private colleges. How is he going to do that without compromising his retirement future? How do his kids' educational expenses fit in the picture with his retirement security? At ***The Safe Money System***, it's very important to develop a retirement plan that incorporates all the pieces of a client's life.

Retirement planning is similar to the art of interior design. The designer has to make the wallpaper of the home fit with the furniture and overall decor of the house. If the owners of the home are a conservative couple that listens to opera all the time, the designer shouldn't recommend polka-dot wallpaper that clashes with their dark-hued sofas, right?

In order to make my investment recommendations fit in with the lifestyles and dreams of my clients, I ask them during the initial evaluation: "Pretend it is three years from now; what do you want to see happen with your finances, career, and personal life that would make you feel good about your progress in those areas?" This question gets them thinking about their goals and values and not about the products I can offer them. In turn, their answers give me a better idea of their parameters and dreams, so that I may recommend to them the right financial products for their retirement. Remember how we talked about how important it is for people to know their limits? It's just as important for their financial advisor to know his clients' limits. Otherwise, how can he create the right plan for them?

The third stage is **Implementation** or execution of the Safe Money plan. I prepare the plan and revise it as desired by my client. At this stage, I put it into place.

Finally, the fourth stage is the **Preservation** of our client relationships. ***The Safe Money System*** is constantly developing ways to give our clients up-to-date information about the financial environment including a blog that I update regularly to keep my clients informed.

Lack of focus is the surest way to kill the planning that will achieve your dreams. It is of paramount importance that my clients are educated and reminded of their desire to stay the course in their Safe Money solution, so that they aren't tempted to return to the Wall Street casino when people around them start bragging about how much they won at the "tables." I need to constantly remind them of what happened in 2007-2009, 2000-2003, 1991-1994, 1987, 1982, and even back in the early 1970s. Client relationships are very important to me, and I want to make sure that my advice is available to them whenever they need it. People need to be reminded that gambling is an attitude that permeates American society. Betting is everywhere: sports, investments, and even odds on who is voted off reality TV shows! If that's your idea of entertainment, fine, but don't let it cross over into the way you think about managing your money!

Okay—now you've heard my clients' success stories and my

successful philosophical approach to investing and relationship building.

What are you waiting for?

It's time to leave your broker with the **"it's not you, it's the uncertain economy"** break-up line and visit us to begin your own success story. I hope to be able to feature your Safe Money success story in the sequel to this book. But that can only happen if you're willing to get out of the Wall Street casino…and stay out forever!

Chapter 10

Money and the Pursuit of Happiness

I grew up as an athlete. I was a quarterback of the football team at one point in school and was a pitcher on the baseball team with a great future ahead. When I was nineteen years old, I was injured riding a motorcycle. What a dumb thing to do—ride a motorcycle—for a kid looking for a major league future! I slid on gravel going head first towards the ground just as a truck was passing around a curve. The truck missed me by fifteen feet. Guess how many times I went back on a motorcycle in the past forty years? Zero. In the same way I evaluate risk and results for my client's retirement planning, I evaluated what could have happened in my accident and what would happen if I got back on the motorcycle. I weighed the enjoyment of the motorcycle against my enjoyment of golf and other sports—or life itself without a crippling injury. Not surprisingly, I decided that I better not get back on the bike.

The story I just told serves to illustrate my philosophy of life that I also share with other people: Know who you are and what your personal boundaries and goals are. Use that knowledge to evaluate your decisions about an investment, marriage, or career. If the information to make your decision is outside the parameters of your dreams or goals, you must decide accordingly. If you do what I just advised, you will have better understanding of yourself and control of your life. What brings you the most fulfillment is an important key to your life. If you are trying to make decisions in which the consequences or results are more than likely outside your area of fulfillment, then don't make that decision. I love the Dos Equis beer commercials with the "World's Most Interesting Man." His advice is priceless: "Those things that you are no good at—do not do those things!"

Don't let the word "philosophy" scare you. I'm not here to tell you what the ultimate meaning of life is or how to live. Nobody has the key to life! I just want to share with you a couple lessons that I learned that have worked for me. Maybe, you'll find these lessons helpful for you.

Let's start with money. How should it fit into someone's life philosophy? I can't say what the perfect perspective on money is, but I know that for me, money is neither good nor bad. To me, money is just a tool. Money can be a tool for business development, a tool that builds a healthy retirement fund, or a tool to give back to society. For instance, I can't personally visit all the homeless shelters in Los Angeles to help the needy people in them, but I can donate money to these shelters. In this case, money is a tool for me to give back to the community.

There are all kinds of ways that our society looks at money.

For example, money is associated with taxation. Most people hate taxes, but others see it as a necessary evil. Essentially, when we pay our taxes, we give the government money to protect us and care for us. Whether we associate money with donation or taxation, in my opinion, it's just a tool to help society run.

There are also people who hoard money with a selfish and greedy mindset. They don't believe in the principle of sowing and reaping. All they know is to accumulate money and never use it to bless other people. At the end of their miserly lives, all they will have is a vault full of money and a garage full of cars without any beneficiaries to appreciate them for sharing their wealth. If those scrooges don't make a decision about how to reposition their money to benefit others, then the government is going to make the decision for them (through taxation), and they will, ironically but inevitably, lose control of their riches. They'll become philanthropists against their wills, and their beneficiaries will be the Pentagon and a whole bunch of government programs they probably spent their whole lives screaming against.

As I understand it, many very wealthy people like the Rockefeller, Carnegie, and the Rothschild families knew the importance of charitable endeavors when it comes to money. To them, money is not just a tool for business; it is also a tool to give back to society.

I grew up with the notion, as did many people, that people with extreme wealth obtained their wealth dishonestly. For instance, the story was that Henry Ford got rich because he exploited his workers. Rockefeller made money because he ruthlessly controlled the railroad transportation of oil, and Bill Gates steamrolled start-up companies with his monopoly in the tech industry. These stories about how rich guys made their wealth might be half true and half false. The sad thing is many people overlook the fact that those guys have given much of their wealth to charity. Gates has his Bill and Melinda Gates Foundation that works on causes like AIDS research. Rockefeller and Vanderbilt both have universities named after them for the support they provided education and research. Carnegie is a legendary name in American philanthropy. These successful people were successful because they could let go of their money and put it to use in a charity or a worthwhile investment that reaped benefits.

For me, a life philosophy about money is ultimately tied to the philosophy of giving and sharing your wealth. Money is a good tool if it helps you share your blessings with others. It's essential to look at money not only as a tool to buy or invest in things but also a tool to give back to your community. This way, you engage in the principle of sowing and reaping. You are not only helping others, but you are benefiting from the joy of helping fellow human beings. Remember that a true measure of a person is not how much he accumulates over his lifetime but how much he gives. The golfer Lee Trevino had a line I love: "What you take with you is what you leave behind."

Now, I'm not saying to give your money to just anybody or any organization to fulfill a life philosophy of giving. My philosophy of knowledge, understanding, and control still applies for charitable donations and bequests. You have to know what organizations help causes that are important to you, and you have to understand how they will use your money to further that cause. This allows you to exert control over how your charitable dollars are spent. If I find out that the organization to which I am looking to donate is funding things that I don't believe in or is exploiting their funds, then I won't donate. I'll just move on to another more effective organization.

I always do research before putting my money into something, and I encourage my clients to do the same. What part of the money they raise goes to the mission, and what part goes to salaries, fancy offices, luxury travel, and other perks? It can be shocking to discover just how "off mission" some charitable organizations can be. For all these reasons, it's important for me in an interview with my clients who want to donate to charity to find out what they are passionate about, what their causes are, and which charities they are familiar with before they write a check to a random organization.

If you are going to think of money as a tool in life, think of it as an arc that describes the path of an arrow. What's the target? How does the money travel along that arc—how does it get to where it's going? Use your money wisely by doing research on how to spend it the most effectively. Don't just throw cash into any investment or charitable organization before you see its fundamentals. Control the arc of your charitable spending. Strike only when ready. Otherwise, you will shoot blindly, miss your target, and might even end up hurting someone.

What Holds You Back from Success?

Let's turn now to a brief discussion of how success and failure fit into one's life. Some people are scared of success. Why? I can tell you the answer from personal experience because like many people, I've been afraid of success. Some people are afraid of the responsibility that comes with being successful. They think, "When I'm at the top, will I always do the right thing? Will I be judged correctly? Will I become a hypocrite? Will people hate me because I'm successful? Will it mess up my kids?"

In answer to those people's worries about being the next Trump or Buffett, I say this: Know who you are. Know your limits as we discussed at the outset of this book. Do your due diligence on your decisions. Ask questions like "Does this decision align with my values?" If you take this approach, success should not be worrisome to you. You'll handle success just fine. If you make your best effort to make the right decisions, you will often do the right thing no matter how successful you are.

In addition, you should be thinking about bringing forth success in your life. Otherwise, you are like the farmer who throws seeds haphazardly into the field without any goal of returns. That farmer will starve his family. You cannot go through life without wanting to be successful at the things you do. The desire to be successful gets things accomplished. Sitting there and doing nothing for fear of success doesn't get anybody anywhere.

There's also the fear of failure. This fear comes from the lack of faith in yourself or in the world. This fear is self-destructive and prevents you from accomplishing the things that you want. I've seen kids fail in their classes just so they do not qualify to play in a sports team. They are afraid that once they make the team, they would disappoint their parents if they ever lose a game. Failure isn't an outcome in these cases; it's a deliberate strategy to avoid an even worse outcome.

It's not only kids who have this fear; adults have it too. Someone might hold on to his money too tightly and not invest in a house that his wife wants for fear of losing money. He can afford the house given his financial situation, but he just doesn't do it. He lacks faith in the economy and in his ability to invest. In the end, his wife leaves him for his fear of failure. Therefore, the fear of failure can lead to decisions that produce destructive results. Fear of failure can bring failure in its wake.

If fear of failure is something that troubles you, as long as you are pursuing the good of the people in your life or the causes you care about, you shouldn't submit to the fear. For instance, you should not decline a job for fear of failing at it if this job could feed your family. Besides, who would hire you if he didn't think you are competent enough to do the job? The fear of failure, like the fear of success, is debilitating. In order to get over these fears, you need to focus on the people you care about and what you can do for them instead of focusing on the fears themselves.

Then there's the question of making decisions and the fear of making decisions, which we call procrastination. Recently, I came across an article titled "Thorough Research Creates Effective Decisions." I believe in the message of those words. Don't let anyone rush you into a decision before you have a chance to research the different aspects of the decision. Buying a refrigerator? Don't grab your wallet before you figure out what size fridge could actually fit in your kitchen or else you might end up returning your new appliance—not to mention the eye-rolling you'll get from your spouse. Don't be hurried into a decision on anything in life based on the perception that the opportunity will never be there again. As I stated earlier, life is full of thousands of new opportunities.

Be patient in your decision-making. In time, patience will reveal any kind of deception going on in a situation. For example, if you are going to invest in a new business venture, wait a little while before you actually put in money. During this time, you might find that the partners in this business venture are inept or that there is something wrong with their business model. Having patience will save your money from going down with a flawed investment. Patience will also save you time. A patient person doesn't have to use extra time to fix mistakes that he made from his hurried decisions. Measure twice and cut once. It's old advice, and it's still effective.

I stressed the "buy when ready" principle in a previous chapter because I know patience and research is important for any kind of decision. You should only jump into an investment or donation when you have done your due diligence (talking to people, looking at statistics, and so on) for that investment. The most important thing you can do when doing due diligence is "know thyself." Know what your financial situation is and how much money you can afford to give, lose, or reasonably gain. If you do that, your investment decisions will yield much better financial results. Based on the preparation that went into your decisions, you can look forward to achieving your desired outcome. You can better predict the results of your decisions by determining how much effort you put into your decisions. Or to put it simply, don't play darts when you're figuring out your life.

Moreover, one decision can teach you about another. One failed decision can lead to a successful decision. For instance, some of my greatest successes came from failures from certain decisions. My failed decisions taught me to not prepare for a decision in this way but prepare in that way. It's like the "W's" and "L's" or the wins or losses observed in baseball. If I know that I trained well all season, then I know that my team can rely on me to bring home the victory. A loss can teach me to train in a different way or to train harder. Defeat doesn't hobble successful people. They take the licking, learn their lessons, and move on.

Develop a Uniform Philosophy

As you have probably noticed by now, my philosophy of life consists of three elements: knowledge, understanding, and control. It definitely makes it easier when you have a philosophy that is consistent all the way through, from your investments to your personal life. When I repeatedly use the term "control," I do not for a minute believe that we have any semblance of absolute control over things in our lives such as health and random things that just happen as a result of living in a world of dysfunction. I am basically using the word control for faith—faith in God as the foundation for my personal philosophy of life.

Let me give you an example of what I mean: You have never driven a car before and are learning the various features and functions of the vehicle. You desire to learn how to stop the car and to control how that happens. Well, you need knowledge of what stops a car, understanding of that knowledge to put it into action, and now you have the control to do what is necessary to stop the car. However, if you don't take the necessary action of faith (your control of the action of stepping on the brake), the car won't stop, no matter how much knowledge and understanding you have of the process.

Faith is Action (control) based on Belief (Knowledge) sustained by your Confidence (Understanding) that what the owner's manual said concerning how to stop the car is true—the ABC's of Faith, if you will.

I try to live my life in faith mode for all decisions I make. I read the Owner's manual (the Bible) to gain the knowledge and understanding of how the "car" (me) was designed to operate and then take the appropriate action to control the outcome God's way by trusting Him at His Word. That's about as simple as I can sum up my philosophy of life!

One of my favorite scriptures in the Bible is from the Jewish Book of Proverbs, again written by the world's wisest and richest man at that time, King Solomon: "Trust in God with all your heart and don't rely on your limited understanding of things. Acknowledge Him in all your ways and He will direct your steps." If it was good enough for the ole king, it's good enough for Randy.

What's this have to do with money, you ask? Well, if you do your homework and come to the conclusion that you're done gambling with Wall Street with your financial future, and you come to an understanding that My Retirement Coach's Safe Money System will work for you like its worked for my clients for 30 years, then you now control your future by taking the appropriate action of getting out of risk into safety (faith in The Safe Money System). It's that simple!

With the Safe Money System, you would make about 7 percent average returns on your savings each year into the future. Sometime in the future, your buddy might tell you that he made 30 percent returns that year. Then he gives you the "look" and asks, "What are you doing with just 7 percent a year? You need to get back in the stock market. What are you, a chicken or something?" Your faith in your decision to use The Safe Money System will allow you to politely brush his suggestion away because you are fully confident that you made the right decision with Safe Money.

Besides, if you average your buddy's gains in the stock market over the past ten years, his gains are probably negative even though he can brag about his 30 percent for one year. Maybe you have to be a chicken to lay the biggest nest egg!

Even though my life philosophy is based on a belief in God and acting on His "Owner's manual," you don't have to be religious or spiritual to understand or follow my philosophy. My favorite song writer and performer John Mellencamp has a song with the message: "You have to believe in something, or you will fall for anything." If you don't believe in anything else, at least believe in yourself to do the right things in escaping the Wall Street casino for a system of security and contentment.

The Next Generation

We've talked about you long enough. Now let's talk about your kids for a moment. Specifically, let's talk about raising children and how to leave our wealth to them. In sharing money with your children, you have to choose to partner up with them or to enable them. Let me illustrate the difference between partnering and enabling with the example of the Rothschild family.

The Rothschilds are a family of merchant bankers in Europe. As merchant bankers, they accumulate their wealth with the arbitrative system: They pay their customers X amount of interest for their deposits in the bank and loan money out for a higher interest rate. In the late 1700s, Mayer Rothschild, the patriarch of the family, had five sons. He needed to figure out a way to have his sons all take part in the family business and share the family wealth. He decided to put each son in a major European capital to be in charge of the family business in those locations. With this arrangement, he taught his children responsibility by making them partake in the family business operations rather than just allowing them to eat of the fruit without any input or effort.

If any of the Rothschild sons wanted money from Dad, they had to borrow from the family bank. They couldn't say, "Dad, I need money" and expect the money to be handed to them; they had to write out a business plan for the money they wanted with an objective, details about the course of business, and how they were going to repay the loan in the future. If the kids wanted the money, they had to earn it. With this kind discipline and the sense of responsibility that Mayer Rothschild instilled in his children, their family's banking dynasty survives to this day.

Mayer Rothschild was successful in distributing his wealth to his heirs and ensuring his family fortune could last into the future. He was able to do that because he partnered with his children by giving them a piece of the family business to manage responsibly.

In contrast to the Rothschilds, let's look at the example of the Vanderbilt family. Cornelius Vanderbilt was a highly successful businessman who amassed enough wealth in the late 1800s to donate a million dollars to Central Tennessee College, which is now Vanderbilt University. Mr. Vanderbilt left money to his descendents with no game plan or strings attached. In other words, he enabled his children to use his wealth without them earning the money.

Recently at the 125th reunion of the Vanderbilt family at Vanderbilt University, the descendents of Cornelius Vanderbilt realized that not one of them at the reunion was a millionaire. One of Vanderbilt heirs said that he saw his father and his grandfather, the direct heirs of Cornelius, have their relationships and marriages broken because of the money issues they had.

Remember the earlier discussion of the futility of pursuing happiness from money? See the difference between enabling your children and partnering up you're your children when it comes to family wealth? Money is a tool, not an end. Happiness based on a contented heart is the goal, not a vast sum of money handed to you without a plan or system in place.

If my twenty-six-year-old son, Brandon, comes to me and tells me that he wants to buy a house, I'm not going to just hand my money to him. I will only give him money under certain conditions. These conditions might be signing a second trust deed for the house after he shows me his monthly budget. And when he refinances his house or sells it, he has to pay me back. If Brandon wants to start a business, he and I both know that 95 percent of all startups fail, so he better work out a business plan for me before I loan him any money to do it. I partner up with my son when it comes to finances. That way he understands that nothing is just given to him. In addition, partnering with him gives me control of not only my own money but also my mentoring to my children on how to manage money while they are young. I'm not going to lend them money to invest in the risky "opportunities" on Wall Street, that's for sure.

My philosophy of life based on faith in God affects my parenting. When my kids were teenagers of driving age and were leaving the house, I would ask them, "Where are you going?"

And they would give me an annoyed look and say, "Out."

Then I would respond, "Well, while you are 'out,' make sure you are driving the car. I don't want you to be the passenger in someone else's car late at night."

The reason I insisted on this was because I had knowledge,

understanding, and control (faith) on how I taught my kids to drive a car and to do it defensively and responsibly. I didn't have the same confidence in other kids' training or skills. Because they demonstrated to me during their first year of driving that I taught them well, I had much peace of mind knowing that if they screwed up, they would be responsible for the consequences, not somebody else's kid. And they have blessed my faith in them with good results!

Furthermore, all three of my sons attended community colleges after high school rather than attending private schools right out the gate (that frankly I couldn't afford for all four years for all three boys at $150,000 each per degree). I needed assurance or knowledge that they were serious enough about their educations to start out at a community college and then work their way to private schools with good study habits. I wasn't going to pay $40k a year for a private college just so they could learn how to open a can of beer their freshman year! Two of the three boys graduated from private universities after attending community college for the first two years, and I gladly paid for their educational experience.

From Money to Marriage

Now let me give my two cents about the marriage relationship. Sometimes, spouses are not on the same page on certain issues in life, such as where to invest for retirement or where to send the kids for pre-school. As if the conflict between two people wasn't enough, we might also have the grandparents chipping in an opinion or two. As a result, we might have four different outlooks on one issue. How do we keep competing outlooks on issues like money, raising kids, and career choices from overwhelming a marriage?

Obviously, in the courting process before marriage, people don't discuss money matters because talking about money can be a deal breaker. In the back of our minds, we might fear, "What if the other person strongly disagrees with my financial or political perspective? Or what if they realize I don't have as much money as they had hoped?" So we keep silent about money before marriage. Keeping silent in the courting process about finances is not always a good thing because a wife might find out a husband's real opinion about how to earn and handle money too late in a marriage.

In a marriage (and only when people ask for my opinion!), I advise that either the wife or the husband (but not both) take charge of the decision-making in certain aspects of life like household management, business planning, and so on. As a result, the wife or the husband who has not been designated the implementer of the plan can be in the role of counselor on the specific issues. In this way, they are a team, but the responsibility to implement the plan falls on one party who is gifted in the administration of the family budget and financial bookkeeping.

I don't believe in joint banking accounts. I do believe in joint savings accounts, but the family budget needs to be handled out of one checking account. You need to know what each of you earns, how much tax withholding and contribution to retirement savings needs to come out of each paycheck, and then each of you put your pro-rata funds into the monthly budget account. You each need to agree on how much each of you can spend (without having to ask your partner) on the basics for the wife (nails, hair, monthly needs of kids' activities, etc.) and for the husband (recreational activities like golf, going to ball games with friends, grooming needs, etc). However, there is nothing sadder in my experience of counseling families for thirty years than seeing one party or the other having to answer to the other on every single dime that they want to spend out of their own agreed to budget limits.

And men—if your wife doesn't work or works part time, you need to realize that you need to give her a monthly, agreed-upon salary for her hard work in running your kingdom at home. Remember that if you don't get that fact now, her divorce attorney will help you understand it later!

For instance, in my marriage, I'm the entrepreneurial type who enjoys the spontaneity of my work schedule, can't work to build someone else's dream or empire, and doesn't want to relocate out of Orange County, California. My wife, Crystal, is a Midwesterner who loves to be in a company environment and thrives in the corporate, team-based culture. As a result, we look at things differently as far as how we earn money and our career choices. Obviously, we can't agree on everything.

So we both have to agree that one of us gets to decide certain household or financial issues and the other one respectfully supports the decisions and implementation of the plan. Somebody has to be designated the leader to make the decisions in their area of expertise or giftedness, so that the implementation of decided plan is carried out successfully. Otherwise, there will be too much conflict, unwanted arguments, and time wasted.

Trust and understanding is essential in a marriage. When I first met my wife, she was a senior-level manager at a technology firm. She also has an athletic son with great professional prospects. I understood that being a mom is more important to her than being a corporate manager, so I told her after she was laid off in the early 2000s tech bubble that she should focus on what is more important to her. I wanted her to trust that I could make enough money for our family so that she didn't have to work. And she trusted me. For six years, she didn't miss any of her son's games or other activities. She could raise her son without placing him on the corporate altar or sacrificing him for her corporate career. She was able to raise her son without a nanny because I understood her needs, and she trusted my ability to handle our family's financial needs with my income.

Currently, my wife works only three days a week as a personal assistant to a wonderful lady who is very charismatic and encouraging. She wanted to apply her administrative skills to some kind of work in which she was passionate as were the people with whom she worked. Our marriage works, and we are content because she is not under a lot of stress from work like she would be if she continued her role as a senior corporate manager with long hours and a daily commute. My wife and I understand each other, we trust each other, and because of the understanding and trust, we love each other unconditionally.

Finally, there are certain decisions in a marriage that are very hard to make when we bring in the issue of money. For example, let's say a young couple who has been married for ten years lives in southern California with two kids. Their support system is here. One day, the wife's company wants her to move to Chicago and will pay her an extra $100,000 for doing so. If money is this couple's god, then the choice is obvious for them. If their values are attached to their support system in southern California, then they need to decline this offer. But what if the family has to move or the wife will lose her job?

Suddenly the decision becomes more complicated. In this case, in order to make the right decision, the couple has to examine their needs and their values. If they need the wife's income, then they will move. If they don't, they can stay in California, and the husband can be the sole breadwinner for a while. It is important to realize from this example that money cannot decide everything in a marriage. It is through careful examination of the values in a marriage that effective decisions are made.

I do investigative background research before most of my decisions in life whether about business, finances, health, technology, or my personal life. I let my knowledge become understanding, and I let that understanding become wisdom. When I apply my wisdom properly, I gain control of my health, wealth, and happiness. As I mentioned earlier in this chapter, control is really faith that this particular action that I'm about to engage in would give me this outcome the majority of the time. If I am unsure of the outcome of my actions, then I am acting out of stupidity or "blind faith."

Thorough research creates effective decisions! Your entire life hinges on the decisions you make. Your decisions will create tragedies or joy. Laughter or tears. Pain or pleasure. Don't let anyone rush you into any decision before you are prepared. Be patient, and adhere to the "Buy when ready" process not "hard sell." Remember that Patience is the weapon that forces Deception to reveal itself.

Understanding of knowledge is not only essential for our actions, but it is also important for connecting with other people. In order to develop meaningful relationships, you have to understand the areas on which you and the other person agree or disagree. Stupidity is when you marry someone you haven't fully understood and therefore trust, then wonder why it didn't work out. I'm very happy with my relationship with my wife and kids because I know and understand them. I took the time to get to know and analyze who they are. This way I can minimize my mistakes when it comes to decisions I make in my relationship with them. Trustworthiness is the single most important trait that you must have to enjoy meaningful and fruitful relationships with our family, friends, and others in the community.

Understanding and trustworthiness are also paramount in the relationship between a financial advisor and his/her client. Some people are afraid to "fire" their financial advisors because they fear their advisors' feelings would be hurt. But they have to understand that their relationships with their brokers are purely professional, even if your broker happens to be your roommate from college. The decision to leave the Wall Street firm is a financial decision, not a decision about friendship. Unless your broker is willing to reimburse you for your recently devastated portfolio so that you can retire in the lifestyle you had hoped for, then it's a business relationship. And you need to make the necessary business decision that lines up with your desire for risk or safety. Again, it's that simple! Okay, I'll get off my soapbox now. I thought you might be wondering, "Who is this Safe Money guy? What goes through his head?" Hope you're not sorry you asked!

Chapter 11

The Truth About Home Equity Management

Most Americans have their financial net worth tied up in two large assets: their homes and their retirement accounts. We rely on this combination to provide us with a pot of money to survive on in our later years. You have probably received advice to pay off your home mortgages as quickly as possible. The idea is that rather than being burdened with house payments at retirement, you'll just sit comfortably on the front porch of your home worry free. However, is having a house free and clear of debt the best way to go?

No. And here's why.

In his best-selling book *Missed Fortune 101*, retirement strategist Douglas Andrew states: "The most important elements of home equity management are maintaining liquidity and safety of principal and creating the opportunity for home equity to grow in a separate side fund, where it is accessible in the event of an emergency:"

For example, a couple comes into my office and asks me to give them counsel on the largest investment of their lifetime. They say to me, "Help us retire securely. What kind of an investment should we make?" Then I give them some features of an investment that they might consider as follows: 1) you can determine the amount of money you put into it; 2) you can set up a schedule of future investment contributions; 3) you can contribute more each month than what's originally scheduled; 4) all the money you put into the investment, however, is not liquid and not safe from loss; 5) this investment earns no returns; 6) your income tax liability will increase with each contribution; and 7) finally, when this investment plan is complete, it would not pay you a dime of income for your retirement. Now I ask them, "Sound good to you?"

"Of course not," says the husband, "who in the heck would make such an investment? There is no liquidity, flexibility, rate of return, or tax advantages. It's against the four pillars of financial planning you talked about, Randy."

Then the wife tugs the husband's sleeve and says to him, "Honey, doesn't that kind of sound like our mortgage?"

Is a Mortgage Good or Bad?

A mortgage is a loan from the bank to finance the purchase of your home. It's bad because of all the reasons my previous example pointed out. Plus, with any kind of loan, there is interest. No one likes to pay interest. Therefore, everyone thinks that the mortgage is your foe because it is debt, and "debt" is an ugly word. Because we think mortgage is bad, many financial advisors advise their clients to invest in homes using the "get-rid-of-mortgage-ASAP" strategy. The myth is that this strategy is the best investment for your retirement.

The truth is that the mortgage does more good than you know. Not only does it help you finance your home, but it helps finance your retirement. I'm going to show you how the mortgage is actually your friend.

The big thing to realize here is that there are two kinds of debt: preferred debt and non-preferred debt. Preferred debt is debt you should have because it gives you safety, liquidity, and a rate of return. The tax advantage you would get on the preferred debt is just the icing on the cake since preferred debt is tax deductible.

Non-preferred debt is the avoid-at-all-costs debt. It is debt owed to credit card companies and other institutions that charge an extremely high amount of interest like 10-20 percent. You can't deduct non-preferred debt. It costs more to stay in non-preferred debt than in preferred debt. You are better off going into preferred debt to pay off your credit card balance.

I put mortgages in the preferred debt category. For example, you want to buy a $500,000 house. You put $100,000 or 20 percent of the purchase price down and take out a $400,000 mortgage from the bank for the house. The bank will charge you about 5 percent interest rate. The first advantage of mortgages is tax deduction. You are in the 30 percent tax bracket, so after the tax deduction, you really pay a 3.5 percent interest rate to the bank. In other words, if you have a $2200 monthly mortgage payment, you really pay $1540 to the bank because of your 30 percent tax deduction. That's a really good deal.

Uncle Sam has become my partner because he helps to defray the cost of borrowing for me by giving me a tax advantage. He's giving me a tax incentive to buy a house in order to boost the economy and give jobs to realtors, builders, contractors, etc. Our economy has gone down the drain recently partly in response to a real estate depression that terminated many housing-related jobs.

Now, I never want people to pay interest on their investments just to get a tax deduction. People shouldn't go into debt unless there is a good reason to do so. I'm going to show you that the reason to have a mortgage goes beyond the advantage of tax deductions.

The Arbitrage System

The prevalent myth nowadays says there are two kinds of people in the world: those who earn interest and those who pay interest. People who earn interest go to the bank, put $100,000 in a CD, and get 2 percent returns on their money. Others pay interest on the loans they take out to start a business or to buy a house.

I say there is a third person out there who both pays interest and earns interest. The interesting thing is he earns interest at a higher rate than the interest rate he is paying. He is his own banker. He does what banks, credit unions, and merchant banks have done for centuries, that is, borrow money at a lower rate of interest and invest it to earn a higher interest rate.

Like the big banks, this third person understands the power of using other people's money. In the banks' case, they make money with your money. For instance, you go to a local bank, put $100,000 on a CD, and get a 2 percent return for the next year. You think the bank's just going to put your $100,000 in a vault? And it's just paying you 2 percent because they feel good about having extra money in the vault? No! They will loan the money at a 5 to 8 percent interest rate to someone who is buying a house or a car or 10-30 percent to someone who is paying for things by credit card and so on. Overtime, the bank desires to make at least 2-3 percent annually on your money. That doesn't sound like much but think about all the people who would give $100,000 to the bank. Their contributions add up to billions of dollars of deposits for the bank. The bank makes a profit by loaning out the billions. This system is called "arbitrage."

Arbitrage is a system that gives you profit based on the difference between what you pay in interest and what you earn in interest. With arbitrage, you borrow on one rate and invest in another rate. In addition to banks, insurance companies also follow this system when they sell you annuities. That is why banks and insurance companies are among the wealthiest institutions in the world. (I'm talking about reputable banks and not the small banks that have failed in the recent economy for making bad loans.)

Having a mortgage also allows you to take advantage of the arbitrage system. You can take out a mortgage with an interest rate of 5 percent and invest the money that you otherwise would have put into the house in a fixed index annuity to collect returns of 7.5 percent. In the end, you will collect positive returns from your investments from borrowing at a net 3.5 percent and receiving 5.5 percent after tax considerations. If you pay cash for the house in the beginning, you will not be able to collect this kind of arbitrage.

Moreover, if you try to pay off your mortgage as quickly as possible, then you put yourself at the mercy of the banker. Let me explain: Let's say you are thinking about paying more monthly on your mortgage than originally scheduled. What if you pay $3,000 instead of the set $2,200 this month? You are basically saying to the bank, "Here, Mr. Banker, here's an extra $800 that I don't need.

You can take it, and don't bother to pay me interest for it. If I need this money back, I'll come to you, and borrow it on your terms by proving to you that I can afford to borrow my own money." Sound ridiculous? Well, that's exactly what that transaction entails.

With the above example, you lose control of the $800—money that you could use as emergency money in the future to pay the bank mortgage. When you pay the bank that extra money, you don't get any extra tax advantages. If you lose your job or a member of your family gets sick in the future, you won't have this $800 anymore to use. You will be forced to go to the bank to borrow back this money. You would have to deal with all of the bank's tedious procedures in order to get this money back. Plus, you will have to pay interest on the new loan that you take out. You were better off not paying that extra $800 to the bank in the first place and instead putting that money in a rainy-day fund.

The Importance of Liquidity

Nothing beats having cash on hand during gloomy economic times. If you lose your job, get divorced, or get sick, it will really bite that you don't have liquid assets. You would be forced to liquidate assets like your house or car—you would have to sell them for cash at fire-sale prices. On the other hand, people who have cash liquidity can slide by emergencies, meet their expenses, and do grocery shopping, unlike the people without liquid assets. Taking out a mortgage and not trying to repay it as fast as you can will give you emergency cash by separating it from your house or removing it from your backyard as I like to say.

Let's look at this example: Bob and John are both age fifty, have good jobs, and can afford a mortgage. They both inherited

$500,000 in cash and are both looking to buy $500,000 houses. John chose to put up $500,000 for his house while Bob only put down $100,000 for his house and borrowed the remaining $400,000. From 2007-2009, the real estate market went down, and home property values experienced losses of up to 50-60 percent in manufacturing states like Indiana, Ohio, Michigan, and New Jersey. In California, where they live, the $500,000 homes that Bob and John have went down "only" 30 percent in value to $350,000. Whose financial condition is now better (or less bad): no-loan John who put every dime he had in his home, or Bob, who put $100,000 down and took out a $400,000 loan?

Obviously, after the market downturn, Bob is in a better financial situation because he has that $400,000 in safe savings to support him in case of emergencies, while John doesn't. If John lost his job and is in major financial need, he might be forced to go to his banker to borrow money. John will say to him, "Look, I'm free and clear of any mortgage. Can I get a loan for these tough times?" The banker doesn't care that John doesn't owe anything. All the banker cares about is whether John can repay a loan. Without any liquid assets or a job, it doesn't look like John can, even though he's got a house free and clear. If the bank rejects his loan application, John's credit score would go down because he could no longer afford his car payment, etc. He would be forced to sell his house in a down market for $350,000 when he had bought it for $500,000. The house might not even sell right away and who knows how long he has to wait to get the cash from the sale.

In contrast to no-loan John, loaner Bob took the extra $400,000 that he didn't put into his house and invested some of it using the Safe Money Strategy. His investment generates 6 percent annual returns, and his mortgage only carries a 3.5 percent interest rate after tax savings. Therefore, taking into consideration his mortgage, Bob actually earns 2.5 percent returns on the money he didn't put into his house. Bob is taking full advantage of the arbitrage system. Plus, if he's ever in need of cash, he can just tap the extra cash that he's got in his savings account in the bank.

Now someone might say, "Great, I get it; the better man here is loaner Bob. But aren't we missing the fact that Bob's got a mortgage payment of $2200 each month while John doesn't?" Well, I would answer that let's not forget that Bob is really only paying $1540 for his mortgage each month because of his tax deductions. But more to the point, would you rather make the $1540 payment each month with hundreds of thousands of liquid and safe assets or make no payment a month but be lacking in cash in case of emergency? Remember that both had jobs and could afford a mortgage.

The above is our basic discussion of mortgages. We will move on to talking about home equity in general. Let's discuss the features of a prudent investment and if home equity measures up to these features. The features of a prudent investment are safety, liquidity, flexibility, decent rate of return, and tax advantages. I say home equity doesn't have any of the above features. Let's talk about these features one by one.

How Safe Is Your Home Equity?

Home equity is defined as the difference between the market value of the house and the value of the loan (market value minus loan value). If the value of your house is $500,000 and you have $400,000 in mortgages, your home equity is $100,000.

If you have a house paid free and clear, and you experience a flat real estate market for 10 years, your home equity would stay the same without gains or losses. However, if you experience a market lost of 30-50 percent (and these numbers are based on reality), then your home equity would be significantly reduced. You just saw the largest asset you own depreciate. Therefore, it's not safe to put all your money in the house. Home equity is not safe from market attacks.

How Liquid Is Your Home Equity?

My mother is seventy-six years old and has two houses. Her Newport Beach house has decreased 15 percent in value but is still worth about $2 million today. Her other house is worth $300,000. She has less than $20,000 in the bank—period! Her total income is less than $30,000.

My mother is old school since she lived through the Depression. She thinks that if she puts a loan on the house, then she is more likely to lose it. As of now, she only makes $2,000 of rental income from the Newport property—which is below market standards—but that's good enough for her. She only earns about 1 percent annual returns from her real estate each year, taxable as regular income. In addition, she has to be responsible for the repairs and maintenance of her houses. My mother sees her house-rich and cash-poor situation with her houses as good post-depression economic planning.

What if my mother has $2.3 million worth of real estate assets and she went to her friendly banker and said to him, "I got all this money buried in my backyard and I have an emergency requiring $200,000 in cash. Will you lend me $200,000?"? The bank would reject her because she had insufficient liquidity and income to pay back the loan. She even says "Heck, I can use some of the $200,000 to pay you back if needed." The answer is still NO. If she needed cash, she would have to sell her properties with huge tax consequences. The lesson from my mother is that home equity isn't liquid and is usually unable to meet your emergency needs when and if you need money.

What's the Rate of Return on Your Home Equity?

If you bought a house in 2005 for $500,000, and it is worth $350,000 today, you not only got a zero rate of return, but you experienced a 30 percent loss. The traditional real estate market experiences a 20 to 30 percent loss every decade or so. It's all a game of supply and demand; when the demand decreases, the prices fall. It takes about ten years to make up a 30 percent loss. The value of your house will have to grow 43 percent in order to get back to its purchasing price. And it's not easy to climb back through a depressed real estate market. We're not even sure how long it will take to flush out the bad loans and the extra supply for homes (due to the lack of ability to buy) in the recent market.

From my analysis of over sixty years of historical data on real estate cycles, it usually takes about six to eight years to get from the bottom of the real estate market to its peak. When can you expect a point of return in these years? The math is simple: Your house was valued at $500,000 in 2005. In 2009, it is valued at $350,000. In 2015, more than likely, the value will come back to $500,000. And how much did you make during those 10 years? The answer is zero.

Home Equity Loans

Want to create more liquidity for your assets or put more cash in your pocket? Besides taking out a mortgage when you first purchased the house, you can borrow against your home equity by taking out a home equity loan from the bank.

I see scenarios like this all the time: A retired couple in their seventies has a $500,000 home paid free and clear, and their only sources of income are around $35,000 from social security and approximately $25,000 from one spouse's qualified plan, or $60,000 annually—pretty good income, as long as one of them doesn't die or their nest egg doesn't lose money! And they have no other liquidity than the retirement plan.

Well, at age seventy-five, the husband dies, and the social security income is reduced to $25,000 annually from $35,000 to his widow. As fate would have it, the retirement plan value that was around $200,000 at few years ago has been deflated by 30 percent to $140,000 by the last three years of stock market performance. She was counting on the $25,000 income payout for another ten years, but it will only last five years, if it doesn't lose any more value. And her $500,000 home has now gone down 30 percent to $350,000. "What happened," she cries, "and what is going to happen to me?"

Well, now we have a widow in her seventies running out of money before she runs out of life! Can Wall Street help her? Will her kids help her? She is stressed worrying about decreasing income and increasing expenses over the next ten to twenty years. What would My Retirement Coach do for her?

We would bring her hope and encouragement!

We would have her get her retirement plan money out of risk and into a fixed index annuity, and it would pay her $15,000 annually for fifteen years, assuming 6 percent average growth.

We would have her take out a $250,000 reverse mortgage on her home (no widow in her seventies wants to sell her home and move away from her comfort zone).

We would have her put $50,000 into an FDIC-guaranteed CD at her bank and create an income annuity for the next fifteen years with the $200,000. It would pay her an annual income of $20,000. And the home value more than likely will be higher in fifteen years for added income and liquidity if she lives longer than ninety years.

What was the result of this plan? Well she now has the $25,000 social security income, plus the $15,000 income from the retirement plan, plus another $20,000 annually from the reverse mortgage proceeds—a total of $60,000! She won't run out of money in five years or worry about having to live on only $25,000 in her eighties. And she doesn't have to depend on her kids helping her with expenses. She is thrilled to death with My Retirement Coach! And this is a true story!

In Addition to Real Estate, the 401(k

Let's say, optimistically, that you have $1 million in your 401(k). If you take money out of it, it's fully taxable. You might be sixty-five years old and plan to take $75,000 out annually for the rest of your life. But if it's not in the guaranteed Safe Money System, who's to say that million dollars won't turn into $500,000 overnight? It's the ole primary need of the return of your money not just return on your money.

Let me ask you a question: In light of all the trillions of dollars thrown overboard to rescue the passengers of the sinking ship "USS Wall Street," do you think income and estate taxes will go UP, DOWN, or STAY THE SAME over the next five to ten years? If you are a company that needs to increase cash flow to survive, and all things being equal, do you need to lower revenues or increase revenues? There's your answer as to where taxes are heading.

For the 95 percent of Americans for which this book is written, you will be retiring on Social Security and pension income—either from a defined benefit plan (core retirement plan of company, state, or government) or a defined contribution plan (in which you contributed to a 401K, 403B IRA or deferred comp. to supplement your other income sources). If your income from all sources exceeds $35,000, all of it will be taxed. If the taxable income exceeds $68,000 as a couple (or $34,000 if single), you are in the federal 25 percent tax bracket.

So let's say you've done a pretty good job at saving, and you have a good pension from the state, government, or company; plus you have social security and income off other investments. Let's also assume you are in the 30 percent combined federal and state bracket and have $600,000 in your supplemental plan (401K, IRA, 403B, etc.). Taking that $75,000 out would give you a net $52,500 to spend because of 30 percent tax deductions. What happens if you are taxed 50 percent when taxes increase? Then you would only have $35,000 to spend—your lifestyle will be greatly affected. The point is that the 401(k) is not reliable, as it is an IRS lien on your retirement future, and you don't know the particulars of the lien as the rules can and will change over the next twenty years (how it's taxed, when it's available without penalty, and other yet-to-be-disclosed tax law changes on the horizon). This is the danger of having only a 401K or other fully taxable pension plan as your primary source of income and a paid up home where the equity provides no additional income to you as taxes and inflation tears into your retirement lifestyle.

I'm a big advocate of reverse mortgages for those people who have all their retirement strategy tied up in their qualified plans and home equity and who face a possible reduction of their lifestyles when (not if) taxes increase, and they have lost a significant portion of their nest egg over the past three years. I suggest to people who are over sixty-eight years old and who have at least 50 percent equity in their properties to look at reverse mortgages to provide a significant increase in their retirement incomes to make up for reductions from taxes, market losses, and potential medical expenses.

The only limitation to this move is that for a couple, the youngest spouse has to be sixty-three or older. All you have to do is to call your bank and ask for a reverse mortgage on your house. Such a move requires no payment to the bank, no qualifying or out-of-pocket expenses; all you need is to keep your property taxes and insurance current. Note that your family or the state has one year after your death to either sell the house to repay the loan you took out or refinance the house and keep it.

Let's look at a couple of examples on how this strategy greatly helped a couple of my clients: My mom is seventy-six and has her primary home in Palm Desert, California; it was worth $400,000 in 2007, but by the summer of 2008, it dropped to $300,000 as the real estate bubble started to deflate. She had less than $20,000 to her name and lived on Social Security and some of my dad's pension, totaling less than $17,000 annually.

In August 2008, I had her take out a $225,000 reverse mortgage to provide additional liquidity to protect her from further declines in her home equity. In her case and in the majority of cases I review for retired folks, having a home paid off is wonderful as long as you have sufficient income to maintain a decent lifestyle comparable to how you lived before retirement. The interesting sideline to the story: Her home value decreased over the past fifteen months to $225,000, but she has all her equity out and no payments; if she had not acted to get the $225,000 out last year to ensure adequate liquidity, she would only be able to get out $110,000 today. She doesn't care what her home is worth—she just knows that she has money for her needs and peace of mind.

Here's another example where a reverse mortgage would make sense. A retired couple (age seventy-five) has a home valued at $750,000 in 2007 with a $200,000 mortgage with a $2200 monthly payment—and not much liquidity other than a diminished 401K account after Wall Street got done with them. By October 2009, the home dropped in value to $500,000, and the retired owner still has $200,000 in mortgage payments. This retired couple should look at a reverse mortgage for about $350,000 to pay off that $200,000 mortgage (and save the $2200 monthly payment) and keep $150,000. I would put $50,000 into the bank for safety and liquidity and create additional income over the next ten years for $1000 monthly with the $100,000 in an annuity. That's a $3200 per month positive swing in their favor!

But what about the children and the estate, you might ask? It's always the kids who complain to their parents who take out mortgages and reverse mortgages as this move affects their future inheritance. Well, I say to those kids that unless they are willing to write a $2000 monthly check to Mom and Dad's retirement for the rest of their lives, stop complaining. Of course, asking that these kids shell out their own money to pay for their parents' expenses might be asking for too much!

The Difference between Wall Street and The Safe Money System

There is a lot of misinformation and abuse when it comes to the way people are advised to manage their home equity. Insurance agents who sell risky variable annuities and the Wall Street bookies cannot talk to seniors about the proper management of home equity to create safety, liquidity, and a rate of return to enhance their lifestyles. Most financial advisors don't have the patience and integrity to advise people to put away 25-30 percent of their money into CDs as there is no commission on CDs. I believe you have to create a proper blend between safe money annuities and CDs or government bonds so that any short-term liquidity needs are met during the first three to five years of your plan for them.

The problem in this country is that there are very few super wealthy people (less than 5 percent of the general populace) who can afford the risk associated with stock investments, and there are too many Wall Street brokers and insurance company agents chasing them down with the "hard sell" process. As a result, the sales guys have to go after people who can't afford the risk. When there is no longer enough wealth to serve the top, the financial industry pushes risk downward onto the masses. After eating the big fish, they go after the smaller fish and leave no meat on the bones. This Wall Street strategy is born out of necessity and greed. As a result, many people who should not have been targeted by Wall Street were. Wall Street has their eyes set on the 401(k) market because the average Joes don't have that much money outside their 401(k) s. Because the 401(k) is so ubiquitous, Joe is left with little choice but to go along with the risk that Wall Street feeds him.

On the other hand, the Wall Street broker could care less about the senior citizen with $2 million in equity on his house and little liquid assets to invest. The senior might as well be homeless and pushing a shopping cart! They don't care about you unless you have liquid assets to risk. Without liquid assets, you are just not their target market. But you still have significant assets to manage and secure in your real estate equity—usually your largest single asset.

The Safe Money System was created to be a counterforce to these Wall Street salesmen and help people who can't afford to lose money. I have stories upon stories from the people I helped. The economy has collapsed around them, their portfolios have gone down with it, and they are thrilled that they have extra income from the mortgage strategies that I have shown them.

I recommend my clients do what I have done myself. Remember the two fifty-year-old gents earlier in the chapter (Bob and John)? When Bob followed my advice, he only put $100,000 down for a $500,000 home, got a $400,000 mortgage that he could afford, had a partner in Uncle Sam (tax savings on mortgage interest), and invested $400,000 into our safe fixed index annuity. In fifteen years at age sixty-five, he accumulated $1,055,000 earning an average 6 percent. That $1,055,000 would pay him out a $75,000 annual income till he's ninety on top of his 401K, social security, and other income. I would take that $75K and pay the $24,000 annual mortgage for the year

($2200 x 12); after he makes the mortgage payments, he would have $48,600 left over to enjoy that he wouldn't have had if his house was paid off. With my Safe Money Strategies, he will have liquidity, flexibility, peace of mind during his working years, and $48,600 additional income for the rest of his life. By leaving the money out of his backyard, he grew his "repositioned" equity for fifteen years and has enough money to cover his mortgage for the rest of his life—sounds like a paid off house to me without the risk of losing equity buried in the backyard!

For every person who doesn't understand the importance of safety, liquidity, and rate of return on your real estate equity, I have found three who get it. If you don't feel comfortable with my take on home equity, yet you believe that the concepts are appropriate for someone you know, please have them contact us or tell them to buy the book.

A Final Word

Real estate entails risk. So when you do buy additional real estate, do so according to your budget. Put as little down as possible and keep your money liquid on a side pot to cover unforeseen emergencies, repairs, and cash flow needs. Never put every dime you have in a house, the stock market, or a limited partnership so that you are able to handle potential financial emergencies caused by a lack of control of your money.

Chapter 12

How TheSafeMoneySystem.com Can Help You

Now that you've seen all the problems that traditional, high-risk Wall Street-style investing entails, you may be asking, "How do I get started on moving my money to safer ground? And who can help me do that?" As someone who has shown you what a brighter day can look like for your retirement, I'm not going to leave you standing in the rain. I created the website SafeMoneySystem.com to help you. SafeMoneySystem.com is different from Wall Street brokerages primarily because we follow the Safe Money System…and they don't!

The retirement planning industry uses two ways to find clients: the "hard sell" process and the "buy when ready" process. Wall Street only uses the "hard sell" process. Here's how it works:

Step 1

Without a clue about your retirement options, you walk into an asset management firm—we could call it Schwab or Fidelity, but we could just as easily call it Gambling With Your Money, Inc. You are relying on someone to guide you in the right direction. You figure that since these people are wearing nice suits and working out of nice offices, they must know what they're talking about. Of course, they don't, but that doesn't stop them from talking or their prospects from believing what they're told.

Step 2

Upon the advice of an advisor at Gambling With Your Money, Inc., you invest in stocks, or stock/bond mutual funds. It doesn't matter what kind of person you are, whether you're rich or middle class or old, young, or somewhere in the middle. As long as you have the money to invest, Wall Street advisors will sell you the same products. Those products are usually stock mutual funds and bond funds. Why? If you've read this far into the book, you know the answer: Those "investments" make the investment bookies and their casinos the most money.

The "hard sell" process takes place anytime Wall Street can take advantage of your lack of knowledge, understanding, or control. It's like walking into a Best Buy without knowing what kind of TV you want to buy, and suddenly the salesman is in your face with a deal for anything from a small HD TV to a complete $10,000 home entertainment system! The salesperson might end up trying to sell the high-end stuff when your needs and budget don't call for that product. But it's not the salesman's fault that you walked into the store completely unprepared and uneducated concerning your needs. Can you see the similarity in how most people buy their investments that will supposedly secure their financial futures?

In the "hard sell" process at Gambling With Your Money, Inc. and other Wall Street casinos, buyers make decisions based on emotion rather than on information that they understand and that fits into their pre-determined needs and boundaries. (And even though they think they understand the information given by the bookie, what happens when what they are given is misinformation?)

How many people do you see at the mall buying supplemental nutritional pills because of mass marketing in health magazines and TV infomercials or on the advice of their "health advisor," Dr. Neighbor? Do you think they've consulted their doctors or health care professionals about what their actual nutritional deficiencies are? Likewise, we all know a person who got too excited about a refrigerator on the showroom floor of Best Buy and bought it on emotion only to realize that his new fridge doesn't fit into the designated spot in the kitchen? He was overwhelmed by the sight of the ice dispenser on the appliance, the sales talk of the sales associate, and the 15 percent-off coupon he found online. What a deal!

Unfortunately, he let his emotions get the best of him and forgot to do the basic research on what size refrigerator would actually fit in his house!

Remember that the Wall Street salesperson has to create the fear in you that if you don't buy his product, then you will lose money or miss the boat on the gains. Even if you suggest to him that you are not interested in the product, he will try to convince you that you are wrong and that you really need this investment in order to secure your retirement future.

That's the "hard sell" process. They're coming at you unsolicited by phone, dinner workshop invitations, or direct mail advertising to sell you stock and bond funds...but they're really selling you out because you have no game plan to deal with the onslaught of information that you're not sure will work for you. But the Coach has a new game plan for you!

At SafeMoneySystem.com, you'll discover that we've created a system that uses a "buy when ready" process. "Buy when ready" means that you are doing things with a plan versus no plan at all. When you come into our "store," you'll already have a plan based on your core values, the things that make you happy and content, and your investment parameters. Your plan objective will most certainly be to keep your money safe while growing your investments for retirement. If you didn't have this plan, you wouldn't have come to us in the first place. You'd be like those people standing outside Gambling With Your Money, Inc. or one of its many competitor casinos, waiting for the doors to open and waving your checkbook at the first bookie you see. That's not you.

The problem that exists in the Wall Street "hard sell" process is that most people don't possess the knowledge, time, and financial aptitude to discern what investment option lines up with their parameters of knowledge, understanding, and control. People need the opportunity to educate themselves at their own paces about their financial goals rather than having a stranger tell them what they need or do not need before they're fully ready to make an important decision.

The My Retirement Coach Safe Money System™ begins with a familiarization process acquired through this book, our website, speeches at conferences, or media interviews. In this way, you gain the information on the strategies and products available to help you decide if our system works with the pre-determined life goals for you and your family.

We are proponents of using the cutting edge technology available to you in this process of familiarization. Do you still get off the highway to use a phone booth to make an emergency call? Do you still drive to the library and look up information on microfiche? Do you still contact your friends primarily by writing a letter and spending 44 cents on a stamp?

Well, welcome to the new frontier of retirement planning education whereby you can use the technology available for your initial contact with us and first appointment (if you desire) in order to save you (and us) time and money. Face-to-face meetings are critical in confirming trust and understanding in the My Retirement Coach process. We find, however, that most people still insist on face-to-face interaction when it is time to review the plan designed specifically for their needs and sign the appropriate forms for the IRA transfer and account application.

When you go to the SafeMoneySystem.com website, you'll find a short video that makes clear we understand your frustration and uncertainty about your finances in this economy and we want to help you escape your worries. In addition, you'll find a series of four, short, one-minute videos designed to remind you of the four pillars of a worry-free financial plan. As we already discussed, the four pillars are as follows: 1) guarantee of principal; 2) flexibility and liquidity of cash; 3) participating in the growth of the stock market without risk; and 4) having a lock-in mechanism to keep your gains without giving them back to the Wall Street casino.

Your visit to our website is the culmination of your understanding of our Safe Money System™; you felt ready to "come to our store." Only when you are comfortable with our "buy when ready" process will you hit the Contact Us tab on our website homepage to begin the journey to a safe financial future.

After you submit your personal information (minimal information like your name, age, zip code, email address, and best phone number for contact), I will immediately reply with a video thanking you for coming to our "store" and remind you that you went to our website for one reason only: to buy safety, flexibility, growth without risk, and the ability to lock-in your gains. You did not contact us to buy mutual funds, bond bunds, stocks, limited partnerships, or anything that could not give you guarantees, control, or a peace of mind. We are not bookies, and My Retirement Coach does not have a gambling license to operate a casino!

After you say "yes" to us, an experienced Retirement Coach who is trained in our system will contact you within 72 hours to find out the following in a brief phone conversation:

- How did you arrive at our "store"? (e.g., this book, a speech, media interview, referral, Google search, etc.)

- What about the Safe Money System™ most pertains to your needs?
- What do you have that needs to be protected from the bookies?

Once we know a little about you, we will ask you a few questions to confirm your understanding of what we do, how we do it, and what we will help you accomplish. We don't make our work rocket science. We keep it simple and concise. All you have to do is fill in the blanks for us, and we will get the job done for you. This "buy when ready" process can happen wherever you are physically located whether in Canada, the U.S., or Mexico, as our coaches are within hours of where you are.

Even after the initial phone conversation, you don't have to leave your home or office when reviewing your Coach's first recommendations concerning your needs. With today's technology and an Internet connection, you can speak to your Coach during a virtual conference while drinking a glass of wine on the phone in front of your home computer! Time is indeed money, and both you and your Coach want to spend more time with family and less time fighting traffic on the freeway. Why not have the convenience of having the preliminary fact-finding meeting over the phone and computer!

Of course you can meet your coach face to face at any time during the "buy when ready" process. The decision whether to conduct the initial familiarization process using computer and phone technology or face to face is your call.

As we get deeper into the initial fact-finder discussion, we will discover whether you need an accumulation solution or an income solution. If you do not plan to retire in the next five to ten years and just want to build up a big pot of cash to live off of when you do retire, then we will create an accumulation solution for you. If you are retired or plan to retire within three years and need a source of stable income with no principal risk, then we will create an income solution for you.

What do we need to know? We'll ask you how long you want to accumulate money before income is needed; how long you plan to receive the income stream after retirement; what your desired retirement monthly budget is; and how much you will receive from various sources like pensions, company plans, and Social Security.

After getting your necessary information during the initial phone call, we will contact you again within a week for a virtual or face-to-face session where we will answer any remaining questions. We will also give you opportunities to help us adjust and fine-tune the financial plan that we have worked out for you.

If you are good to go with the purchase of your customized Safe Money System™, you'll sign the appropriate documents for the annuity, life insurance, US government bond fund, CD, IRA, or other savings vehicles that we have recommended to you. Then, we will notify the appropriate custodians of your plan to initiate a tax-free transfer to your new IRA or another savings vehicle. Your new IRA custodian will usually be a major insurance company and/or FDIC-insured bank that offer the Safe Money products you desire for your future needs.

You and your Retirement Coach will also sign an additional conformational disclosure. This disclosure is basically a checklist that assures us that we accomplished everything we had set out to do for you. It's part of our mission to do the best job we can do. This disclosure will go to the database of a trustworthy marketing agency which has an established relationship with the insurance industry and with which we have worked with for years.

Keep in mind that your money will never be transferred to SafeMoneySystem.com. We must all avoid the Bernie Madoff Syndrome by never writing a check to a sales organization or a marketing company or any of its agents. Where there is no control of your money, abuses can easily happen. People wrote Bernie's company a check, and he never put it into the bank or a mutual fund. Always have the check made out to the FDIC-insured bank or insurance company!

Our retirement service to our clients doesn't stop at the transfer of their money. We continue to inspire, inform, and educate our clients about the latest news in the market, so that they can keep up with what's going in the financial world. We do this by a blog, videos, ongoing seminars, and excellent customer support. Questions from clients on taxes, estate planning, real estate, insurance, and so on will continually be answered by the Retirement Coaches. Your business with us is not a cold and impersonal transaction but the development of a long-term relationship with a caring organization you can trust with your money.

My son Brandon, who is our Director of Technical Operations, has the perfect analogy on why we keep things simple: If you can't explain to your twelve-year-old child what your financial need is and how we will solve it, then you don't have the knowledge and understanding to move forward. (Of course, smart kids like yours will be thrilled that you are securing your financial future without risk and with peace of mind!)

SafeMoneySystem.com is successful because we help our clients focus on where they are—not some imaginary financial dreamland where they don't currently reside! We have the inventory of products to secure our clients, and we will take care of the product if there are any problems. But it is up to our clients to partner with us to identify their needs so we can pick the right solutions for them. Remember that we created the Safe Money System to replace the risky guessing games of the bookies!

The Final Call

So what's it going to be? Will you call up a brokerage house like Gambling With Your Money, Inc. for the "hard sell" process, or will you visit our store at SafeMoneySystem.com for the "buy when ready" process?

Let's review. If someone who has not read this book calls up a brokerage house and says that they need some advice, what kind of advisor are they going to get? Will it be an experienced Retirement Coach trained in the Safe Money System™ founded on my three decades of experience in retirement, tax, and real estate planning or a Wall Street bookie ready to peddle some risk options off the casino's gaming menu? The bookies can help you answer some basic questions, but they have not in the past nor are they now able to put together a plan that will keep your hard-earned money safe.

If you are concerned about safety, the bookie's usual option for you is a balanced fund, long-term corporate bond fund, or a government securities fund. A balanced fund is essentially a mutual fund that consists of a combination of supposedly conservative stocks (an oxymoronic term at best) and safer bonds; in theory, a balanced fund is less risky than a mutual fund that consists solely of stocks. But what these brokerage house salesmen are recommending to you is putting lipstick on a pig (the phrase they use to describe those investments...behind your back).

Balanced mutual funds dropped 30 percent in the recent downturn—not much different from most mutual funds that dropped over 50 percent at the March 2009 lows. It's like when you walk into a casino, instead of playing the dollar slots, the casinos have arranged for you to play nickel slots. You think, "Hey, I won't lose as much playing nickels compared to dollars, right?" I've seen my mother play on the nickel slots, and she'll lose more money playing on those slots as playing on the dollar ones—it just takes a little longer!

Likewise, you can lose just as much money investing in balanced funds as regular mutual funds depending on the allocation of your total funds; it's just a different game on the Wall Street casino menu. These bookies are not going to recommend a fixed index annuity or CDs, which are safe alternatives—that's not what they're paid to do. The responsibility of the brokerage house salespersons is to keep your money in the casino in stocks and mutual funds so they can collect fees and commissions whether you make money or not.

Take one of my long-time friends as an example; he has $250,000 in a bond fund. Recently over lunch, I asked him to explain the basic features of the fund to me, but he couldn't. I asked him if there are any guarantees that his money will be safe, and he answered, truthfully, "I don't know." You and I both know the answer is probably not. Sadly, his situation is like most Americans who have their money tied up in investments that they don't understand. They only bought into these investments because their brokers said to do so. I told him that if he can't explain to his

13-year-old daughter where his money is and if it is safe, he's in the wrong deal. Then my friend said to me, "You know, you're right!"

If you come to SafeMoneySystem.com for your retirement needs, then you are telling us that you can't afford to lose any more money and you want a secure and peaceful retirement. I've already told you about the Safe Money System™ formulated based on my thirty years of real world experience. You expect from us an objective analysis of your wants and needs—followed by a safe solution. You didn't come to our store just to browse, did you?

Visiting SafeMoneySystem.com is like visiting Nordstrom as opposed to a "99 Cents" store. When you walk into Nordstrom, you already expect high-quality service and high-quality products. You are well aware that the coat you want to buy today is going to last you a lifetime because it is well made. Moreover, you like the associates there because they respect the customer. On the other hand, many people walk into a "99 cents" store just looking for something cheap without knowing what they want. They end up buying a bag full of low-quality products that will last them a week and that they don't really need. SafeMoneySystem.com is a successful retirement consultancy for the same reasons that Nordstrom is a highly respected and successful retailer. My best client is an educated buyer as opposed to an uncertain prospect who isn't sure what he wants from life and retirement planning.

In contrast to Wall Street brokerages, SafeMoneySystem.com does not call you every five months to say that your investments have made returns of 5 percent, and now it's time to move the money into another investment vehicle. That's like telling you that you've made some money already in the slots at the casino, and now it's time to move it to the blackjack table. The big brokerages live by the velocity generated from moving money from one musical chair to another. They want to create the illusion that if you are not moving with them, then you are losing out on some gains. Well, SafeMoneySystem.com is not interested in illusions, and we certainly have no interest in fueling people's desire to gamble their money away.

SafeMoneySystem.com helps you determine your boundaries for your personal and financial needs, and we will work within them. One of the first things we are going to ask you is what you think your life expectancy is. For us, it doesn't seem proper to give a sixty-five-year-old person a thirty-year plan when he has a family history of relatives only living until they are eighty. In this case, the personal boundary for the retirement income needs for this sixty-five-year-old is his life expectancy. Each person's boundaries are different depending on whether he/she is married or single, has children or not, and whether there is the possibility of taking care of an elderly parent's needs. Another consideration for determining your retirement needs is how important it is to leave a financial legacy to your grandkids or church/temple. SafeMoneySystem.com respects those boundaries and feels that it is imperative that those issues be addressed in the process.

Of course, there's a lot of competition in the retirement planning industry. If you search "retirement planning" on Google, you get about 4 million hits. How does SafeMoneySystem.com stand out? Well, I doubt very much that our prospective clients will be convinced by a Google search to want our help without the benefit of reading the book you're holding or the other familiarization tools mentioned earlier. Moreover, you came to us for help—we didn't call you up cold like a salesperson to tell you, "I have a system, and you need to hear about it."

How do people find out about SafeMoneySystem.com? Our clients do not find us through the Yellow Pages. They find us because they were exposed to our Safe Money System™, and its message of "enough is enough" resonates in their hearts. My hope is that more people will hear me, catch the Safe Money wave, and join us at SafeMoneySystem.com… and find the peace of mind and the retirement wealth they deserve.

Since we primarily served public servants for thirty years (teachers, police, fire, government employees, and doctors and nurses at non-profit hospitals), we see ourselves as a servant to public servants. Our clients believe in our Safe Money System™ because they have seen and experienced the results we've given them over the last 30 years.

I created the SafeMoneySystem.com brand because it is very identifiable and relatable. Everyone needs someone to guide or coach them through their retirement planning decisions. Our target audience is the average person like you and I who makes a decent living and wants a peaceful, contented retirement. When people come to us, they already know what we do and what we can offer them with our retirement strategies. For them, it's like walking into Best Buy to buy a TV and already knowing the type of TV that they want: a HD Sony 42 inch. They know what they want, they understand the product they desire, and they control the buying process—if they don't get the price they want, they'll go to another store.

The same is true with our clients: They know that we will give them the knowledge, understanding, and control that they can't find on Wall Street to create the retirement lifestyle of their dreams.

Those who prefer risk over safety are not our target audience.

The audience for SafeMoneySystem.com is typically a person over fifty. They are consulting with us because they are tired of Wall Street's casino games founded on a gambling mentality. They might have gotten so used to hearing that a Safe Money System™ isn't a possibility or that they can't accumulate wealth using CDs and annuities, that they are led to believe that our system is too good to be true. Now they have the proven mathematical results contained within our system as proof that Safe Money with peace of mind is not only possible but is absolutely imperative for contentment in this life!

Chapter 13

In Pursuit of a Successful Philosophy of Life

There's a reason why some folks did not open their quarterly statements: The fear of seeing negative numbers on a page all started for them during that 20 percent stock market drop in July and August of 2008. When the drop occurred, people began asking, "What about that Safe Money thing I heard about? Maybe it's time I do myself a favor, and grab a lifeboat before the Wall Street ship sinks." Those who were smart enough to consider this visited SafeMoneySystem.com, and the rest was history.

After the July/August 2007 fiasco, things only got worse for the next two years; the S&P Index would drop another 40 percent. Yet, My Retirement Coach's clients weren't feeling the loss one bit. From 2007 to 2009, many of my clients had account statements that showed an increase of 10 to 15 percent on their money without any decrease in principal. This increase included the bonus that insurance companies gave them from signing up for the annuities that I recommended. During the last two years, I would ask my clients, "Are you feeling pretty good about making money while protecting money?"

And they would answer, "I have $550k in my retirement account now. Had I kept my money in a mutual fund, I would have $370k today. So, yeah, I'm feeling really good!"

None of them had any losses on their retirement accounts over the last ten years! My clients followed my strategy of transferring money out of stocks and mutual funds into the safety of CDs and annuities and my advice to extract money from their houses in the forms of mortgages, home equity loans, and reverse mortgages to create liquidity. I showed them how to take advantage of the arbitrage system by taking out a mortgage at one rate of interest, investing the money to earn a higher rate of returns, and earning the difference. As a result, if they ever come across an emergency like a job layoff or disability, they will have money in their pockets to take care of it. They won't have to go to the bank and beg to borrow their own money because the banker doesn't think they can repay it.

I also deterred my clients from making bad decisions for their retirement funds. If someone was tempted to buy a house in foreclosure down the street for a quick "fix & flip" as seen on TV, I told them, "Don't do it." The reason why is that my client needed to keep money liquid and not put it into a risky investment. I teach my clients to keep 20 to 30 percent of their money liquid in CDs or government bonds so they can handle any unforeseen issues in their lives. If that client had put his retirement money into buying another home without the knowledge, understanding, and control necessary to survive an overheated real estate market, he would have thrown money away and reduced his life expectancy from the ensuing stress. In the following, I'd like to share with you some stories about the success my clients achieved with the Safe Money System.

Success Stories

Before coming to me for advice in September 2007, one of my clients, a man we'll call Sam, had $600k in his 401(k) account with his company. He was hit by the July/August 2008 stock market drop, and his 401(k) account went from $725k to $600k. When that happened, he couldn't open his statements anymore.

Sam was sixty-three and wasn't sure when he would retire or get laid off—it could happen in the next three or four years. He was referred to me by a best-selling author on retirement strategies who was also a networking partner with My Retirement Coach. Sam visited our website and believed in my message that losses more greatly affect one's retirement than gains do. He knew that he could not afford to lose any more money, and it was time for a strategy other than gambling.

During our initial evaluation interview, he told me that in addition to the safety issues about his 401(K) plan that he had been advised to borrow on his house and buy more property. This was September 2007! He already refinanced his home, so I told him to take the money, put it into CDs at his bank, and forget the gambling mentality on buying in an overbought market. I also told him to move his 401(k) money into two fixed index annuities by doing an in-service distribution from his 401(k) from his employer to a self-directed IRA with the insurance company as custodian. (As mentioned earlier, an in-service distribution is a tax-free plan for people older than fifty-nine and a half, where you can move your money from a 401(k) account to a self-directed IRA while still working at your company.)

Sam followed my advice and moved his money into two $300,000 annuities that gave him 10 percent in upfront bonuses and secured his principal and retirement future. Two years later in October 2009, his retirement accounts are worth $660,000. He made no gains over the past two years, but he also lost nothing because of the annual lock-in feature of the annuities. He was really happy about earning nothing at a time when his colleagues (who were not my clients) lost 30 to 50 percent in their retirement portfolios. If he had left his money in the 401(k) account at the brokerage house (per the advice of the 401(K) plan representative), his account would be worth $420,000 today. He would have $240,000 less in his retirement account if he had not given My Retirement Coach the opportunity to help him secure his retirement future.

Three years ago, Tom and Anne were referred to me for retirement coaching. Anne was sixty-four and a retired travel agent who had recently beat cancer; Tom was sixty-eight and retired from the ministry. They had no money in the bank, but they had $100,000 in their IRA account and $600,000 buried in their backyard (equity on their free and clear home). That's it. Social Security was only going to replace 35 percent of their income from their working years.

They had followed all of the advice offered by a well-known Wall Street guru: Pay off your home as soon as possible and put money into your IRA. They followed that advice and now faced a real problem. They had no liquidity, reduced income, and a paid-off home. You've heard the term "house rich/cash poor"? Well, that description fit them to a tee.

They did not want to sell their house and move to a smaller home in order to have additional cash to create more income. So I advised them to reposition the money out of their house and create a Safe Money retirement plan. They borrowed 60 percent of the house value and created a $500,000 interest-only mortgage. Next, they put $75,000 of the proceeds into CDs and $425,000 into annuities. The goal was to provide a pot of money to pay the mortgage and give them an additional $30,000 annual income until Anne turned eighty-five. You can see the logic behind that advice, I'm sure. Their equity in the backyard was not giving them any income.

The CD paid the mortgage and income for Year 1. They were paid a 10 percent upfront bonus on the annuity principal and received 11 percent of the 15 percent growth of the S&P Index during their first year (mid 2006-mid 2007). Overall, they made 21 percent returns on their money in their first year with me and saw their $425,000 grow to $515,000. In 2007-2009, they made nothing, but they also didn't lose anything.

In addition, I advised them to remove the $100k in their IRA from exposure to stock market risk and put it into safe investments. Instead of that $100k being worth $70k today if the money was unmoved, it's now worth $120k. The result of this plan: they have an additional $30,000 income after paying their $24,000 interest only mortgage for the home equity repositioning, plus another $5,000 annually from their IRA—for the rest of their life! Plus, they have Social Security and part-time income!

By the way, the couple's house went down in value by 25

percent, but they didn't care (and they shouldn't care with the safety net they created for themselves with My Retirement Coach). Remember, they don't want to move! The stock market went down 35 percent, and they didn't care because all of their money was safe from stock market losses, even though they participated in the gains of the market. On average, they made 7-8 percent annually over the last three years in this recession. Unbelievable? Believe it! Tom and Anne were very happy with the results I gave them.

I have another client from Nashville; Elena was married to a highly paid executive and has two teenagers. Elena was forty-six when she received a spousal IRA rollover for $600k in divorce settlement money in early 2007 and deposited it with a well-known Wall Street brokerage firm. In July-August 2007, she watched her $600k nest-egg decrease 11 percent to $530k in the first stock market sell-off. She was told by the Wall Street bookies to hang in there and that the market fundamentals were strong long term.

When she was referred to me in August 2008, the $600,000 had decreased 15 percent in eighteen months to $507,000; I told her to get her money out of the risk of the stock market right away. She could not afford to gamble with her financial future! I told her that the real estate bubble was ready to pop to the detriment of the overall economy! (This was right before the October 2008 financial meltdown. I don't want to make you think I have some magic crystal ball—anybody with half a brain in his head saw that real estate was on the verge of a historic collapse.)

Elena took her money out of her brokerage firm to the distain of her broker who vehemently protested the Safe Money annuity strategy. Why wouldn't he be opposed? No more fees in his pocket for churning her account! I advised her to take $100,000 of her

$507,000 and put it into a CD at her bank as an IRA. This gave her the liquidity she might need over the next five years.

She put the remaining $407,000 of her IRA in a fixed index annuity with one of the largest and most financially sound insurance companies in the world, Allianz Life. With Allianz, she got an initial 15 percent bonus plus a 3 percent guarantee for Year 1; her guaranteed value after one year was $480,000. She wasn't going to tap the money in this policy for another fourteen years. With just 6 percent average annual gains from her policy, she could accumulate $1,100,000 in fourteen years and be set for life. She could also take money out of the account for emergencies if needed. Best of all, she wasn't incurring risks anymore. She could sleep well at night, knowing that her money was growing, not shrinking.

If Elena had kept her money in the brokerage, her $507,000 balance would have gone down to $300,000 by March 2009 from the stock market decline and recovered to $400,000 over the last six months. With the help of My Retirement Coach, her IRA accounts total $585,000 with no risk of decline after the recent strong recovery and economic uncertainty.

Before she withdrew money from her brokerage, her broker kept telling her that it was the wrong thing to do. He told her that she was young and could afford to take the risk in the market and regain her original balance. The broker had to tell her this in order to keep her money under the control of his brokerage house. Well, so much for all that nonsense she had to go through! She's now almost $200,000 ahead without the stress of worrying about her money during the last year. She learned that "enough is enough" and that she will have over a million dollars when she hits age sixty and be set for life!

Another client, Ann, experienced a success story that I wish for you as well. She was sixty-two when I was referred to her in July 2006 and worked in real estate. She had two large assets to her name: her non-qualified account at a brokerage firm for $440,000 and her 401(K) account at her company worth $250,000. Both accounts were in stock mutual funds in July 2006.

Ann accepted my advice to get out of risk; at this stage of her career and life, she couldn't afford to stay in the casino. She moved her $437,000 to a fixed index annuity with Aviva Life, another strong insurance company I recommend. Today the account is worth $525,000—a 20 percent increase since July 2006. Had she stayed with the advice of her broker, the account would be worth $300,000 with the 30 percent decline in the market over the last three years.

I also advised her to do an in-service distribution of her company's 401(k) plan to move her money out of risk into safety with another fixed index annuity in 2006, but she waited a whole year before doing so. Yes, her $250,000 grew from July 2006 to July 2007 by 15 percent to $287,000. Again, I met with her and reminded her that now at age sixty-three and with the real estate market very shaky that she could ill afford losing any money.

Thankfully, she finally took my advice in July 2007 (right before the market collapsed) and did the in-service distribution to an IRA with Allianz Life with the $287,000. Today her account is worth $330,000. Had she stayed the course with risk, her account would be worth $200,000 at the Wall Street Casino. Yes, she's very happy with the peace of mind, as she gets ready to retire this year at age sixty-five. I saved her from over $300,000 in losses over the last three years on her accounts by recommending the Safe Money Strategies I want you to follow.

One of the themes in this book is to ask your financial advisor how he or she invests to ensure that they're not saying one thing and doing something different. So let me share with you my own approach to financial planning for my wife and myself. It'll show you that I put my money where my mouth is!

Our house had almost tripled in value over the last ten years here in southern California. Back in 2006, my wife and I took $300,000 out of our house in the form of a new mortgage and used $100,000 to improve the house. I also put $200k into a properly structured life insurance contract so that I had a pot of money growing tax-free for the next fifteen years, which will give us tax-free income to pay 100 percent of the mortgage plus an additional $50,000 annual income at that time. We also now had additional liquidity, flexibility, and control over our money that the equity buried in the backyard did not give us.

Three years after taking out that mortgage, my house went down in value by 25 percent—a decrease of $250k. When that happened, I didn't care what the house was worth; my mortgage payment was still the same as it was before the equity repositioning as I have an interest-only loan (why pay principal to the backyard, right?). I believe the real estate market will be higher in fifteen years, and I like having my money available to me without having to sell the home or beg the banker for a loan on my own money in the backyard if I need funds during the next ten to fifteen years.

My wife also did an equity reposition on her separate property rental condo in late 2006 (which had also tripled over the last ten years). She took out $160,000 and created her own bucket of safety with another life insurance contract that will provide additional retirement income for her as well as additional safety and liquidity over the next twenty years. By the way, the interest-only mortgage is covered by the rental income as we don't need a taxable positive cash flow at this time while our incomes are sufficient.

Given what we now know about where real estate and the stock market were headed, it's fairly obvious that my wife and I made the right decision! The message here isn't that "Randy's so smart" or "Randy's so fortunate." The message is that I invest the same way I advise my clients to invest. I follow the same strategies I preach to my clients. Does your Wall Street bookie invest in what he's peddling to you over the last ten years? If so, your broker…is probably broke!

A Safe Money Kind of Guy

These days my clients are opening their statements, calling me, and thanking me for getting them out of the Wall Street casino. Better yet, the majority of my clients aren't calling me; that's good testimony that they are satisfied with my work for them. They feel no need to tell me that they are scared, nervous, or worried. There are no sleepless nights for me or my clients.

It's different, of course, for people who are still in the market. In the current economic environment, what are the Wall Street brokerage firms advising people whose retirement accounts have been devastated by losses over the last two years? You guessed it: Stay the course. Put even more money into your 401(k) and other qualified plans in order to recover your losses. They are basically telling their clients to double down on the blackjack table. Sure, as always after a huge devastating decline in the stock market, there has been a recent positive correction. But remember what you are focused on: no more gambling!

Wall Street advisors are not giving their clients guarantees or even sound advice that will protect their nest egg from another potential catastrophe; they are giving them uneducated and far-fetched guesses as to what may happen in this economic mess over the next few years. They are asking the rabbit to move over in the hat so that they can pull some numbers out for the client.

As a Safe Money kind of guy, I formulate educated recommendations based on reality, not whim. As a result of my research, I know that the stock market indexes give historical average annual returns of 7 to 8 percent, and the real estate over time yields average returns of 5 to 6 percent annually in the traditional growth markets like California and the Northeast (and around 2 to 3 percent growth for most of the country). When brokers promise that they can get returns higher than those numbers, I view such "advice" with a skeptical eye and know to keep away. By now, I hope you'll feel the same way I do.

When I make an investment or advise my clients to make an investment, I make sure that I know what mathematically is going to happen in the short haul and in the long run. However, I also keep in mind that nothing is certain except uncertainty. Even with knowledge and wisdom, a person will never be operating with 100 percent certainty. But I do the best I can to stay informed. I have very low to non-existent risk tolerance. That's why I left Wall Street in 1983.

I feel sorry for the guys who are still peddling Wall Street's risk, toiling away behind their trading desks and following the recommendations of their immediate superiors and their firm's executives and analysts. The misinformation they have received over the last twenty years has caused their clients much heartache and loss. These people, contrary to what some may believe, don't lack a conscience. They have to feel bad about how terribly they've blown it for the people who came to trust them. Of course, they haven't figured out an alternative to keeping people locked into risk. I empathize with them, but I don't exactly respect the fact that they lack the imagination to offer any other kind of advice. They may feel bad for their clients, but they're still lining their pockets with their clients' money in the form of fees and subjecting their clients to even greater losses, fears, and frustration.

When a cyclical bubble hits the economy every five to seven years and stockbrokers lose their client base, they have to scramble for new clients and begin the whole risk-laden process with a new set of prospects. The brokers don't control the loose underwriting and the fuzzy accounting that goes on at their brokerage's headquarters, yet they pay the price for losing their clients' money. The financial advisors are the public faces of their brokerage house, and they are forced to keep their faces down in shame because they let the clients who trusted them down.

Most Wall Street brokers (and that includes me almost thirty years ago) have no intention of misinforming people. Believe me, very few people go to work in the morning thinking, "How am I going to screw with people's money today?" Unfortunately, for all the good guys out there trying to do their best to make their client's money, there are also crooks like the Bernie Madoffs of the world. The unscrupulous advisors, using the "hard sell" process, would say, "Well, if I don't sell this guy this stock of questionable value, someone else will." That's like a drug dealer, in justifying his evil activities, saying, "If I don't sell this kid drugs, someone else will." Advisors who rationalize that no one has a gun to their clients' heads when they accepted the risk in the stock market are foregoing their primary responsibility to ensure people don't lose their nest eggs by advocating safe money strategies.

Again, I know that many financial advisors have good intentions at heart for their clients. If they could make money for their clients without the risk, they would do that any day. That's why many advisors are interested in doing transparent, safe, and honest retirement planning work using our Safe Money System. Like me, they want to get referrals for a job well done, not for a sale well made.

My dream is to expand the My Retirement Coach movement nationwide and talk about the Safe Money System and the contentment my clients enjoy on programs like Oprah, Ellen, or Dr. Phil—- maybe even Larry King! Educating and bringing hope to Americans devastated by Wall Street's shenanigans would not only be a blessing to people looking to retire securely but also a blessing to financial advisors who are looking to work for the good of society and escape the stress of peddling risk in the Wall Street Casino.

Four Strategies for Successful Relationship Building

So how do the relationships between client and My Retirement Coach differ from what goes on in the Wall Street Casino? I'm glad you asked! I have four strategies for Client Relationship Management that made the success stories that you just read possible. They are Education, Evaluation, Implementation, and Preservation.

Let's first discuss Education. My clients found me; I didn't hunt them down. They attended an educational workshop, visited our website, read about me in an interview in the media, or were referred to me by satisfied clients. The Safe Money System and the fundamental beliefs of our company resonated in their hearts. So in the first stage of my relationship with my client, I educate them about safe investments and about the system of risk on Wall Street.

The second stage is the Evaluation of the client's investment goals, parameters, and their lives in a broader sense. I want to help people discover a personalized strategy for their money that fits in with their goals and values. For example, a father makes $200,000 a year and is highly taxed. He has to figure out how to put four kids through college in the future, including giving them the option of going to private colleges. How is he going to do that without compromising his retirement future? How do his kids' educational expenses fit in the picture with his retirement security? At My Retirement Coach, it's very important for us to develop a retirement plan that incorporates all the pieces of a client's life.

Retirement planning is similar to the art of interior design. The designer has to make the wallpaper of the home fit with the furniture and overall decor of the house. If the owners of the home are a conservative couple that listens to opera all the time, the designer shouldn't recommend polka-dot wallpaper that clashes with their dark-hued sofas, right?

In order to make my investment recommendations fit in with the lifestyles and dreams of my clients, I ask them during the initial evaluation: "Pretend it is three years from now; what do you want to see happen with your finances, career, and personal life that would make you feel good about your progress in those areas?" This question gets them thinking about their goals and values and not about the products I can offer them. In turn, their answers give me a better idea of their parameters and dreams, so that I may recommend to them the right financial products for their retirement. Remember how we talked about how important it is for people to know their limits? It's just as important for their financial advisor to know his clients' limits. Otherwise, how can he create the right plan for them?

The third stage is Implementation or execution of the Safe Money plan. I prepare the plan and revise it as desired by my client. At this stage, I put it into place.

Finally, the fourth stage is the Preservation of our client relationships. SafeMoneySystem.com is constantly developing ways to give our clients up-to-date information about the financial environment including a blog that I update regularly to keep my clients informed.

Lack of focus is the surest way to kill the planning that will achieve your dreams. It is of paramount importance that my clients are educated and reminded of their desire to stay the course in their Safe Money solution, so that they aren't tempted to return to the Wall Street casino when people around them start bragging about how much they won at the "tables." I need to constantly remind them of what happened in 2007-2009, 2000-2003, 1991-1994, 1987, 1982, and even back in the early 1970s. Client relationships are very important to me, and I want to make sure that my advice is available to them whenever they need it. People need to be reminded that gambling is an attitude that permeates American society. Betting is everywhere: sports, investments, and even odds on who is voted off reality TV shows! If that's your idea of entertainment, fine, but don't let it cross over into the way you think about managing your money!

Okay—now you've heard my clients' success stories and my successful philosophical approach to investing and relationship building. What are you waiting for? It's time to leave your broker with the "it's not you, it's the uncertain economy" break-up line and visit SafeMoneySystem.com to begin your own success story. I hope to be able to feature your Safe Money success story in the sequel to this book. But that can only happen if you're willing to get out of the Wall Street casino…and stay out forever!

Chapter 14

Some Final Thoughts

By now, you know me pretty well. You know what I believe about investing. You know how I feel about risk in general and about the way the Wall Street casino peddles risk, taking advantage of investors' fear (and greed) and their desire to look good and sound cool at cocktail parties. You know how I feel about the importance of sleeping soundly at night because your money, retirement, and future are safe. You know my spiritual core and my thoughts about how money fits into a balanced life. You even know that I take my own advice and that my wife and I utilize the same Safe Money System that I advise for our clients at My Retirement Coach.

Although we've never met, I know a lot about you—simply because you've read this book all the way to the end. I know that you're a hard-working person who takes your responsibilities in life seriously—at work, at home, and in your financial life. I know that either you or people you know well have been burned by

Wall Street and that you've witnessed tens or even hundreds of thousands of hard-earned dollars vanish once the music stopped. I know you've always believed there was a better way. I'd like to believe you've found it now.

Many people may never invest with My Retirement Coach, and I understand that fact. You can't be all things to all people. As we've discussed, I'll never attract the get-rich-quick types, the people who go from infomercial to seminar, waving their credit cards at the "gurus" who may not know how to enrich you, but they sure know how to enrich themselves. The penny stock pickers, the day traders, the people who think they'll make a fortune trading stock options or buying and flipping foreclosures (at the same time that people who actually know something about real estate are going bust)...they're not in my sights, and I'm not in theirs.

But you're different. You're too smart to fall for the hype. I've deliberately written this book in a straightforward, down-to-earth, easy-to-understand manner because the concepts I've sought to share with you in these pages are exactly that: straightforward, down to earth, and easy to understand.

Risk is bad.

A loss is more dangerous to your overall financial health than a gain benefits you.

If you don't have understanding, knowledge, and control over your money, than someone else does. And he's more likely to make profits himself than help you.

The market doesn't just go up. It goes down, and when it goes down, it takes the hard-earned money of many good people with it. The brokers live to sell another day, but you don't have another twenty years to make up for the money you can lose in a matter of months.

As an investment philosophy, discernment beats fear and greed every time. It was true in King Solomon's day, and it's equally true in ours.

If you can't explain an investment to your twelve-year-old, then you shouldn't be making that investment.

Wall Street's system is for accumulating money…and it fails desperately at preserving and distributing it to the people who need it.

When it came time to take responsibility for the loss of trillions of dollars of investor wealth, Wall Street blamed everyone but itself. "Trust us," they said. But when the market collapsed, Wall Street's tune changed. It became, "You should never have trusted us."

You're probably thinking, "If this stuff is so obvious, why doesn't everybody preach it?" And by now, you know the answer. There's more money for Wall Street in keeping the status quo of tapping into people's fear and greed, so they can tap into their pocketbooks. A commission here, a fee there…it all adds up to money out of your account and into their pockets. Where do you think they get the money to pay themselves those obscene salaries and bonuses? From thin air? No, from hard-working people like you!

By now, you also realize just how passionate I am about working with people like you to protect your investment and keep it safe, so that you can count on the money now and in the future.

I hope this book has been a blessing to you in solving your need of securing your retirement future, without Wall Street's risk. Your intention to have your assets protected needs your action to do so.

If you would like one of our endorsed Retirement Coaches to contact you anywhere in the U.S., or if you need further information about **The Safe Money System**®, please visit us at:

www.thesafemoneysystem.com

My Retirement Coach, Inc.
28202 Cabot Rd. #300
Laguna Niguel, CA 92677

Phone: 949 365 5670

Email: info@thesafemoneysystem.com

15068591R00127

Made in the USA
San Bernardino, CA
13 September 2014